AF271224

FINDING THE RIGHT PATH

Jan S. Doward

Pacific Press Publishing Association
Boise, Idaho
Oshawa, Ontario, Canada

Edited by Bonnie Widicker
Designed by Tim Larson
Cover photo by James Ferry Photography
Typeset in 10/12 Century Schoolbook

ISBN 0-8163-0938-8

90 91 92 93 94 • 5 4 3 2 1

CONTENTS

Why Do We Act Like This?

When I was a very small boy, mud puddles seemed super attractive to me. Not only did I enjoy running right through them, but I would stomp my feet and watch the water splash. My pant legs would get wet, but I didn't mind. I was having fun—and having fun in mud puddles was the most important thing in my life right then. I couldn't seem to get enough of mud puddles, so I would sit down right in the middle of a big puddle and splash with my hands. Just when I was really getting into the action, my mother would always show up.

"What are you doing in that mud puddle?" she would ask.

I was having fun, but she invariably came along to cut off all that enjoyment. I never liked what came next. Mom would drag me into the house all soaked and dirty, strip me of my wet clothes, and give me a sharp spanking on my bare skin. For a moment this held my attention, and I forgot all about the sheer fun of the mud puddles. Next would come the vigorous drying and dressing in fresh, clean clothes, which would be followed by a warning in tones I was supposed to understand.

"Now, young man, I want you to be a good boy. Don't play in mud puddles again. Do you hear?"

With eyes still brimming with tears, I would nod my head, indicating that my hearing was just fine. I promised faithfully I would not do the mud-puddle stunt again.

Once outside, I discovered that the mud puddles had not moved. There they were, right in the driveway—just as I had left them. They looked so good to me. I would walk around and around them, thinking of how much fun it would be just to stamp my feet in the middle of one. Maybe just a little stamp would be OK. The longer I looked at the puddle, the better the idea seemed. Suddenly I would give a big stamp with my foot, and the water would splash. The splashing water thrilled me through and through—and before I knew it, I was right back in the middle of the mud puddle again, sitting there splashing with my hands. In spite of all that had happened, I would recycle the whole affair.

Several years later, when I had outgrown the mud-puddle urge, I looked back and laughed at all my baby stuff with a feeling of superiority. Now I was almost as tall as my father, and I felt so big and so strong. Those feelings seemed to increase daily. I would stand in front of a mirror and flex my arm muscles just to see them bulge.

Now I loved my dad very much. We were the best of friends, but suddenly one day a feeling of macho might struck me. I wanted nothing more than to test my own strength against his. Without warning, I began dancing around him in the living room with my fists clenched.

"Come on, put 'em up! Let's go a couple of rounds!" I challenged.

I figured that Dad might take a swing, and I would duck and show him just how fast I was. I felt so strong and quick that it seemed nothing could stop me.

Dad looked puzzled for a moment as I kept bouncing on my toes and urging him to respond. What happened next was stunning. Like lightning his right hand reached my chest. "Aw, sit down!" he said as he gave me a little push.

Before I knew what had happened, I was sprawled on the floor. Then, quick as a cat, Dad rolled me up like a mummy in the big scatter rug by the piano. My arms were tightly pinned to my sides; only my head protruded from the rug. As Dad straightened himself and walked away, he called to Mom, "Come get your son!"

How embarrassing! To have my own mother release me from this rug cocoon was too much. Here I was the capable one with the ability to do just about everything for myself—and Mom had to come unwrap me! For several days after that I remained somewhat humble. At least I thought I behaved decently. Then one afternoon those strange smart-aleck feelings sneaked up on me again. I really felt cocky. Not only that, but I felt dirty too. I knew I needed a good scrubbing and felt sticky and awful all over, yet in my mood, nobody was ever going to make me take a bath. I lived in a neighborhood where getting dirty and staying dirty seemed to be a status symbol. One boy who lived not far from my house had reached the height of achievement in this area. He owned a horse and rode bareback a lot. His pants were so stiff from horse sweat that they could stand by themselves. In fact, he actually had to climb into his Levi's from a stool. Even if I had owned a horse, my parents would not allow such foolishness. But I was determined that day to come close anyway.

When Dad passed me in the hall, he stopped and whiffed.

"Son, you need a bath," he said quietly.

"Nope! I'm not takin' any bath!" I declared emphatically.

Dad raised his eyebrow. "Well, now that is an interesting announcement."

"Nobody can make me take a bath!" I reemphasized as I thrust out my chin.

"Oh, is that so?"

"That's so!" I said as I put my hands on my hips.

"Well, you are taking a bath, my boy."

Since we didn't have a shower, he promptly walked into the bathroom and started running water into the tub. When it reached the level of the overflow drain, he turned off the water. I was still in the hallway with my hands on my hips.

"I'm not takin' a bath!"

Dad was very calm and cool. He always was, and that made me nervous inside—but I didn't want him to know it. I knew I would be in the tub before long, whether I liked it or not; still I stubbornly stood there.

"I'm counting to ten, and on the count of ten you will be in the tub," he said firmly.

When he reached ten, I expected him to start undressing me, but instead, he swiftly lifted me off my feet and dumped me—clothes and all—right in that tub. Water sloshed all over and even shot up my face and nose. While I sat there soaking and fuming, it occurred to me just how uncomfortable it is to take a bath while wearing clothes. My soaked socks and shoes didn't feel so good either.

Dad didn't say another word but walked away, leaving me to think about the whole matter. The longer I thought, the more angry I became, until finally I dashed from the bathroom to the basement, grabbed Dad's new ax, and rushed outside to throw it deep into a big thorny berry patch by our driveway.

Then something happened to me inside. I felt absolutely awful. I was so sorry for throwing Dad's ax and sorrier I had been so stubborn and stupid. Tears came to my eyes as all the frustration emerged. Why did I act like this? Why did I keep recycling such behavior when I knew better?

The answer, of course, is sin. We come into this world packaged in selfishness and ready to disobey. We want our own way right from the start. We scrap and struggle to maintain our rights. Place two babies in a crib, give them one rattle, and you know what will happen before long? They'll be beating each other over the head with it!

Even worse, we very early start blaming others for our mistakes. I remember sitting down at a picnic table with several children. Everybody was waiting patiently for the food to be passed, when suddenly a two-year-old boy got impatient. He reached his chubby little hands as far as they could extend to grab the cookies. Without regard for anyone else or for anything in his way, he stretched his hands for the stack of cookies. In the process he spilled the tall glass of milk in front of him.

"Oh, Kenny!" his grandmother exclaimed. "You should be more careful!"

Kenny pulled his hands back while the milk flowed around the dishes in front of him. His lower lip began to stick out.

"It's peoples that make me bad," he pouted.

Well, it wasn't "peoples" at all but simply his own childish impatience. Watching Kenny, I realized that day as never before just how early we begin blaming others.

God never intended it to be this way. He never wanted any of us to feel upset, angry, frustrated, or sad. He did not want us pointing fingers at others for our own mistakes. He created Adam and Eve perfectly happy and placed them in the beautiful Garden of Eden totally free from disease, destruction, or death. But Adam and Eve chose to pledge allegiance to Satan instead of God—and the whole world was plunged into sickness, sorrow, disease, and death. Satan lied about God. He succeeded in making it seem that God was holding back some special knowledge by forbidding them to eat the fruit of one tree. Out of Satan's "bargain" they received a knowledge, all right—a knowledge of guilt, which was precisely the knowledge that God in His great love did not want Adam and Eve ever to experience.

Once Satan had Adam and Eve on his side of rebellion in sin, God had to act fast. Quickly angels were sent to block the way to the tree of life. The devil hadn't counted on that; he had assumed that Adam and Eve would eat fruit of that tree and be sinners forever. But God would not permit this.

Although the tree of life was well guarded, there was sorrow all over heaven. The angels realized that Adam and Eve were lost and that every baby born on planet Earth would be doomed to grow up in a world of misery, sickness, and finally death, with no way of escape. People would live out their little lives, die, and go to the grave to stay forever. It was terribly sad.

Enter God's Grace

How to get the human family out of this deathtrap was a great problem. But amid the gloom in heaven, Jesus assembled all the angels. He had a most important announcement to make. He presented the plan that He and the Father had worked out long before the creation of the world. It was a plan that would allow people a way out.

The angels rejoiced to hear this plan, but when Jesus explained the details, they were shocked. Jesus Himself would have to go down to earth and finally die.

This was unthinkable to the angels. They volunteered to go in His place, but Jesus explained that this was impossible. Since the law is as sacred as God Himself, only someone holy could pay the penalty for breaking it. Sin came with such a high price tag that it would cost the life of Jesus. Not just an ordinary death, but the kind of terrible separation from God that the sinner will feel if he is eternally lost.

In Boston's Museum of Fine Arts hangs a large picture of Adam and Eve leaving their garden home. The painting is divided into two parts; one light, the other dark. On the right side, sunshine brightens every tree, shrub, flower, and stream. Even the sunlight filtering though the great shade trees has a special radiance as it strikes the beautiful grass. In the middle of the painting, however, a cavelike exit leads toward the darkness beyond. Clothed in animal skins, Adam and Eve have just entered the shadows and are walking, heads downward, away from happy Eden. A snarling dog lurks in the shadows. The trail leads directly past a waterfall, whipped to spray by the force of a gathering storm. Looking at the picture, you sense something of how sad they must have felt.

But Adam and Eve took with them a bright promise that would glow even in the deep shadows east of Eden. That promise was Jesus. Even though the devil could now tempt and annoy them anywhere in the world, the Saviour would one day come and live among us and by His death finally crush all evil. Like stamping on the head of a poisonous snake to kill it, Jesus would at last destroy Satan and all he stood for. In the meantime, all those born on this planet would need God's grace to turn away from Satan's temptations to sin and to live like Jesus. Grace is part of the bright promise and means God's undeserved or unearned favor. Without God's grace we would never feel sorry for our sins nor ever have faith or hope. It would be impossible for us to repent or to believe or to look forward to a better life without God's grace. So when you begin to say the Pathfinder pledge, "by the grace of God," you are really saying that you need the Lord every step of the way.

Of Pigs and People

One day while walking along a country road, I passed by a lovely hillside pasture with a winding stream flowing down at one side. Pausing to watch the stream for a few minutes, I suddenly noticed some movement in the mud by the stream bank. Right in front of me were heads poking out of the mud. The bodies were buried. Nothing was visible except the tell-tale snout, eyes, and ears. Immediately I could tell they were hogs wallowing deep in the mire. Their contented grunts and snouts told me that they really preferred this filthy ooze to the nice barn on the top of the hill. The farmer may have supplied them with fresh, clean straw, but they wanted nothing more than the dirty, soft mud.

Watching the pigs wiggle around in that mud reminded me that some people, like pigs, enjoy dirty things. When we say someone behaves like a pig, we usually are referring to their eating habits. But people can be like pigs in their choice of wallowing in the sights and sounds of filthy things. These people fill their minds with impure words and stories, music and pictures. They choose the mud and scum instead of things that are clean and good.

The world we live in contains much filth, but we don't have to choose it. Bible prophecies predict that, just before Jesus returns, the entire world will be focused on evil and impure things as they were in the days of Noah before the Flood. In those days, sex, vice, and violence were everywhere. God said this sort of thing would be repeated in a uniquely concentrated manner just before the end of the world.

Today magazines, newspapers, television, and movies flood the marketplace with all sorts of dirty suggestions, foul words,

11

and obscene pictures. The popularity of using sex for entertainment and for selling products—from tires to toothpaste—seems acceptable and normal. One can see impure things night and day. The devil has planned it this way. He would like to keep alive the lie that filling the mind with filth is fine. Making trash tempting is part of Satan's evil design.

Have you ever figured out how he does this? It's a trick called imitation. First he finds some attractive people—like actors or actresses, singers, dancers, or athletes—and uses them as role models. By keeping their personal lives out of harmony with God, the devil knows full well that these so-called stars are really misfits for heaven. By using the stars for models, the devil knows that others will imitate their words and actions. This creates a taste for trash and keeps the vicious cycle of sin moving.

Do you know what happens next? It is not enough for the devil to get many following evil; what he wants is persecution of those who stand for purity and right. Satan gets the imitators of the bad to tease and make fun of those who won't tell dirty stories, see the same videos, or hear the same stimulating music. He wants nothing more than to create the idea that following Jesus is old-fashioned or odd. The last thing the devil likes to hear are the words of Jesus, who exposed him by saying, "When he lies, he speaks his native language, for he is a liar and the father of lies" (John 8:44, NIV).

Jesus Himself said, "Blessed are the pure in heart: for they shall see God" (Matthew 5:8). That word *blessed* means "happy." The happiest people on earth are those who have chosen to be very selective in what goes into their minds. The really happy people are very careful about what they see and hear because they realize that when the mind is polluted, there is no possibility of knowing or loving the Lord. Pollution of the thoughts takes away not only the desire but the ability to love Him.

One of Satan's best-kept secrets is his full awareness that real happiness comes from knowing God and His Son, Jesus Christ. The devil doesn't want anyone finding the source of real happiness. That is why his entire program depends on distraction. "Look! Look!" he shouts as he dangles some new rotten thing. "Don't read the Bible or study anything that will help you find God. Just watch all the smutty diversions I can give you. Be like the hogs in the mud. Enjoy the filth!" And millions look and listen to what the devil sells, totally distracted from finding the truth.

Sally's Two Testimonies

When you say, "By the grace of God, I will be pure," you are saying much more than that you are trusting in God for a clean mind. You are asking that God will give you the right motives as well. Impure motives always make us do and say things just to have approval or to get something we selfishly want. Pure motives help us choose to do what is right because it is right.

Sally sat in the pew next to her girlfriend during the closing part of a week of prayer. She only pretended to be interested; her real interest was herself, clothes, and boys. She knew some of the teachers talked about her behavior, so as she listened that evening, she had an idea. One by one the other students were going forward to testify, and Sally figured it would be very impressive if she did too. Getting up from her seat, she walked down the side aisle and joined the line that formed beside the microphone. When her turn came, she took a deep breath, smiled sweetly, and said, "This week of prayer has meant so-o-o-o much to me. I just want everyone to know how much Jesus means to me."

As Sally returned to her seat, her eyes met her girlfriend's, and she winked. "That oughta impress 'em," she whispered.

But the longer she sat there smugly reviewing her insincere testimony, the worse she felt. She knew that many others who were testifying were honestly telling the truth. The quiet little voice of God's Holy Spirit gently kept speaking to Sally. She knew that she was wrong, that her motives were impure.

Suddenly Sally stood up, and, to the astonishment of her girlfriend and all the others, she went right back to the microphone. Taking the stand in her hand, she gripped it tightly. For a moment the entire church was silent as everyone leaned forward to listen. What was Sally doing up there the second time?

"All of you know I was up here before," she said softly but with deep emotion. "I came up here not only because everybody else was doing it but I wanted to impress the whole school. It didn't take much nerve the first time, but," and her voice broke slightly, "I want you to know that standing here this time is hard, because, you see, I really do need Jesus. I really do!"

The whole student body sitting in the church that evening remained hushed. This was real. This was in earnest. And this was the truth. Quickly a few others came forward to repeat their testimony—this time with the right motives. Sally had shown the way in finding the meaning of "pure in heart"!

Lindsay, Crutches, and Snowballs

Remember when you were six years old? That may be too far back in the dim past for you to recall, but if you look at some first graders, you'll notice something about their teeth. The baby teeth are disappearing, and for a while, before the permanent teeth come in, there usually is a big gap. I want to tell you about two smartly dressed little six-year-old girls with gaps in their front teeth who came to church one spring day.

One little girl wore bright ribbons in her hair; the other wore a brand new spring hat. Their missing front teeth caused them to lisp, and any conversation at close range usually meant getting sprayed.

The girl with the ribbons in her hair walked right up to her girlfriend to make an important announcement. "The memory verth for today ith, 'Be ye kind one to another,'" she quoted smugly.

Her companion shook her head. "Ith not either!" she lisped back. She knew the memory verse from Ephesians 4:32, but didn't understand the word *ye*. Setting her jaw squarely she shot back. "Ith, 'Be E kind one to another'!" And as she said this, the little feather that angled so cutely from her hat danced in unison with her shaking head.

The girl with the ribbons stepped closer to the girl with the hat.

"Ith not either! Ith 'Be ye kind'!"

"Not either! Ith 'Be E kind'!"

" 'Be *ye* kind'!"

" 'Be E kind'!"

Little Miss "Be Ye Kind" became so angry that she yanked off her challenger's hat, threw it to the floor, and stomped on it. That did it! Miss "Be E Kind" hit and scratched in return. Those little girls knew the words to the memory verse, but had no understanding what the words "Be ye kind one to another" really meant!

Big Time Billy and Cousin Scott

Saying "I will be kind" is one thing, but putting those same words into action is really what the Pathfinder Pledge is all about. Billy and Scott were cousins and came to Pathfinder meetings ready to say the pledge and law just like the rest. It was no problem for them to parrot the words from memory, but when the Pathfinder Club went on a picnic, things were different.

Both of the boys were good in sports—and they wanted everyone else to know it. Billy thought of himself as some big-time athlete, and his younger cousin wasn't far behind. They liked to show off and to dominate whatever game they played and were not interested in helping their teammates learn to play better.

Both boys arrived at the Pathfinder Club picnic with baseball mitts and caps all ready for action. They tolerated the sack races and other games, but what they wanted most was to get out in the field and play ball. Finally everybody gathered out at the baseball diamond for work-up—much to Billy's disappointment.

"Aw, let's have teams and really play ball!" shouted Billy.

"Yeah!" added Scott, "let's get goin' on sides. We've had enough of this stuff."

Billy and Scott grinned at each other when they were chosen to be on the same team. This was it! Now they could show off their ability to both their rivals and their own teammates.

It so happened that tall, lanky Ken was on their team too.

The part of Pathfindering he enjoyed the most was hiking and exploring things in nature. Sports were not very high on Ken's list of priorities. He had enjoyed the picnic up to this point; it was fun jumping around in gunnysacks and trying to run a three-legged race. Everybody had laughed and had a good time. Now that they were all playing ball, he figured he would just do his best. He felt fine until his turn came at bat. With Billy and Scott standing by the backstop shouting at the opposing team, he felt nervous. What if he couldn't hit the ball? He tensed as he walked up to the plate.

"Hey, batter, batter!" shouted someone from the other team. Ken gripped the bat and determined to do his best. When the first pitch came, however, he swung late.

"The way to go!" shouted someone on the other team.

Ken felt bad, but he expected teasing from the opposite team. What he hadn't expected was the harsh words from behind the backstop. Both Billy and Scott were criticizing him.

"He sure has a wimpy swing," Billy said loudly to Scott.

"Come on, Kenny. Give it all ya got!" Scott shouted sarcastically.

The next pitch was on its way, and Ken leaned into the swing with all his might. But his swing was far too early, and he whirled around with the bat still in his hands.

"What is he doing? Trying out for the ballet?" Billy snickered.

"No. He thinks he's a helicopter!" Scott gasped in between laughs.

Waiting for the next pitch, Ken was so tense he felt as if his nerves would snap. This wasn't fun at all. As he swung, the ball whizzed right by him and smack into the catcher's mitt. The team in the field shouted for joy. But the words of Billy and Scott were not in fun. They were mean and insulting.

"Who taught you to play ball? Your baby sister?" yelled Billy.

"Why don't you try out for Pee-Wee league?" Scott taunted.

Ken dropped the bat and walked away. He wanted to get as far away from the ball field as possible. When the Pathfinder leader found him, Ken was seated on a log in the woods all alone with his head in his hands. Putting an arm around Ken's shoulder, the leader tried to encourage him.

"You are someone special, Ken. Never mind what others say."

With tears streaming down his face, Ken told the Pathfinder leader, "No, I'm no good. That's what they said. I'm worthless. No good at all."

"That simply is not the truth, Ken. Billy and Scott's words were unkind. Remember that you have special talents. Don't pay attention to other people's cutting words."

The Pathfinder leader had a serious talk with Billy and Scott later that day. After all, what is the use of memorizing the pledge and law if we do not practice what it says at a picnic or any place else, for that matter.

Kindness to God's Creatures

When we are truly kind, even the animals and birds will be aware of it. Part of the pleasure of heaven will be enjoying animals that are totally unafraid of us. But even right here right now we can enjoy a little sample of what those pleasures will be like.

Right next to my house are two bird feeders. All year long my winged friends come and go, bringing with them their sweet songs and special little habits of feeding and flight. In the fall and winter especially, the gray jays come when I whistle. These beautiful light-and-dark-gray birds eat out of my hand. If they think I might have more bread, they will even sit on my shoulders and wait to see if I just might have more.

Knowing that the gray jays are not interested in the birdseed I put on the feeders, I usually go out with some bread before breakfast. If I get there a little late, the jays will be waiting for me on the fence. If I get there a little early, I whistle a two-tone whistle; in a few moments they will be coming toward me in their long, gliding flight. Now I would never be able to enjoy these birds if I were mean and cruel to them. Kindness to animals does have rewards now. The animals' response to kindness also gives us a little window into what heaven will be like when the animals and birds will be unafraid of people.

Lindsay, Crutches, and Snowballs

For a while it didn't seem possible that Lindsay would be able to attend school in the fall. Besides other injuries, bones in both legs were broken and would take months to heal. She had been visiting at a friend's house the day a natural gas explosion shattered the building. It was a miracle she was alive.

When school began, though, Lindsay determined to be there even if she did have to hobble around on crutches. Her pleasant smile and buoyant attitude even encouraged others. Lindsay's close friend and roommate, Diana, was happy to help her in opening doors and carrying books or whatever else would make life easier for Lindsay.

Later that fall a storm roared down from the north and dusted the campus with snow. When even more snow followed freezing temperatures, walking became terribly treacherous. One false step, especially on the slippery sloped walkway, could send your feet flying right out from under you. For Lindsay, it was painfully slow getting to classes on crutches. As she inched her way along the worst part of the walkway, Ronald appeared with an armload of snowballs. He had been pelting others on their way to classes, but when he spied Lindsay, he knew he had an easy target.

"Please don't!" pleaded Lindsay.

But Ronald had packed the snowballs so hard they were now like ice, and he wanted to use them. Without thinking of the consequences, without thinking of the cruelty, he let the first snowball fly. At such close range, it struck Lindsay's crutch and knocked it out from under her, causing her to fall to the ground. He was just getting ready to throw another snowball when Diana saw him.

"Stop! Stop!" she yelled. "Can't you see Lindsay's hurt? That's mean!"

Gingerly Diana hurried as fast as she could across the snow to reach Lindsay and help her to her feet. All the while she kept shouting at Ronald.

"Don't you dare throw another snowball, you hear?"

Once Diana had Lindsay back on her feet again and had brushed the snow off her coat, she strode right up to Ronald. Her face was flushed. Her eyes flashed.

"You've got to be a real coward to do a stunt like that! What kind of a meany are you anyway? That was so cruel! Why don't you go pick on someone with a chance to throw a snowball back at you? Huh?" She paused to catch her breath. "Don't you ever do anything like that again!"

Ronald gulped. He hadn't expected to be told off like this. Dropping the hard snowballs, he sheepishly turned and walked away, leaving Diana standing there with her hands on her hips.

Often people quote an old saying, "Silence is golden." That is true most of the time. It is easy to speak out of turn or say the wrong thing at the wrong time. Remaining silent is usually the best rule. But silence isn't always "golden." Sometimes it is just plain yellow! When we are afraid to speak in defense of the defenseless, we are being cowardly and unkind. Diana showed her bravery that cold fall day by being kind and protecting Lindsay.

The King Who Showed Kindness

One of the customs centuries ago was the ruler's right to kill anyone from a former monarchy who might be a threat to him. Even today, rulers in some countries still follow this custom. The Bible tells us of a king who did not follow this custom but instead showed a kindness that helped to establish himself as a wise ruler.

When David became king of Israel, he would have been expected to take revenge on anyone left in the house of Saul. After all, it was King Saul who had hunted David like some wild beast. After many hard years of fleeing for his life and hiding in caves, it would have been natural for David to seek revenge on Saul. Instead, he allowed the grace of God to shape his thinking. When he learned of Saul and Jonathan's death on the battlefield, he wept. In his grief he wrote a special song expressing a deep and genuine sorrow for both Saul and

Jonathan. You can read it in 2 Samuel 1:17-27. When David was finally established as king of Israel, he had a question to ask his counselors. "Is there anyone left of Saul's family? If there is, I would like to show him kindness for Jonathan's sake" (2 Samuel 9:1, GNB). David remembered how close he and Jonathan had become as friends and his special promise to take care of anyone left. A servant of Saul named Ziba was finally found. When questioned by David he said, "There is still one of Jonathan's sons. He is crippled" (verse 3, GNB), he told the king.

Poor Mephibosheth had been crippled in his feet ever since his nurse dropped him while fleeing from the Philistines when he was only five years old. Mephibosheth had probably been worried when David became king and stayed out of sight on the east side of the Jordan River.

When Mephibosheth finally was brought in before King David, he realized his life was at David's mercy. The king could have ordered his execution according to the custom, but instead, he showed him kindness and offered Mephibosheth a room in the king's palace and food from his table for the rest of his life. This beautiful story told in 2 Samuel 9 is well worth reading.

David acted in kindness in spite of the custom because he wanted to please God.

Copying Satan's ways is natural. If someone trips you and sends you sprawling, the custom is to turn against him quickly. "I'll get even with you! I'll trip *you*! Just you wait!"

Satan delights when we want to retaliate. Whenever that temptation comes, send a quick, silent prayer to heaven; God will give you the strength to overcome. More than that, He will show you just how to treat the people who hurt you.

Listen to the words of Solomon. "If your enemy is hungry, feed him; if he is thirsty, give him a drink. You will make him burn with shame, and the Lord will reward you" (Proverbs 25:21, 22, GNB).

God's better way was demonstrated years ago in the United States Army when a soldier knelt by his bunk to pray one evening. It is most difficult to keep a Christian attitude while constantly hearing dirty language in the barracks, but this soldier knelt as he had always done. Another soldier saw him kneeling there and under the meanness of Satan's temptation picked up his own combat boot and threw it across the barracks at the kneeling soldier. The heavy boot struck him on the back of the head. It really hurt, but the soldier kept right on praying. After lights were out that night, he did what Jesus would do under similar circumstances. Nobody saw him, nobody heard him.

The next morning the soldier who had thrown the boot discovered that both his boots—now cleaned and polished—were beside his bed. Coals of fire!

He felt ashamed and sorry for what he had done. That kind act turned him to repentance and led him eventually to become a Christian too.

I WILL BE TRUE

How Debbie and Sandra Got A's

Of all the girls in the eighth-grade class I taught that year none seemed to get more consistent A's than Debbie and Sandra. These two excelled in every subject. They acted like twins, yet they were totally unrelated. Debbie was a short brunette and Sandra, a tall blond. Their friendship was cemented in similar interests, not looks or blood. Their pleasant smiles and cheerful attitude, coupled with their scholastic ability, made them a joy to have in my class.

That joy turned to sadness at the close of the school year. It was my practice to call every student of mine into my office and have prayer with them before the summer vacation. One by one they would come to share their plans and say goodbye. During the last week of school that year, Debbie appeared at my office door very sober. During prayer she started sobbing, which was most puzzling. When we got up from our knees, she fought back the tears.

"Is there something you want to talk about?" I asked.

She shook her head. Then turning, she hurried out of my office.

More students came, and I almost forgot the incident until Sandra's turn came. She, too, was not her usual self. She didn't sob during prayer, but afterward her eyes were filled with tears.

"What could be the matter?" I wondered.

I didn't have long to wait. Soon both girls returned to my office.

23

"We need to talk to you," Debbie said softly.

I smiled and pointed toward a couple of chairs in my office, but the girls decided to stand instead.

Sandra's eyes were still brimming with tears.

"We've been cheating," she said soberly.

I swallowed, my throat went dry, and I could think of nothing to say in reply to the stunning announcement. I thought perhaps these nice girls had cheated on their final exam in only one class.

"Yeah," added Sandra, who now began to cry. "It was awful. We really cheated."

Then Debbie blurted it all out. "We cheated the entire year!"

Here were two lovely young ladies standing there with their heads bowed, sobbing out their sorrow over their dishonesty. They were certainly intelligent enough and capable of doing well in their subjects, but they had chosen to cheat—and right then their conscience was speaking to them. The girls had cheated themselves out of a full knowledge of their subjects, and out of a genuine open relationship with their classmates, their teacher, and their God. Worst of all, they had cheated themselves out of the peace that comes only by being really true and honest.

Our next prayer session together was one of deep repentance for the girls. Tears that turn people back to a right relationship with God and others can turn to tears of joy. Both Debbie and Sandra really understood this when they left my office that day.

The Curse of the Schemer

If there was one thing that Mike knew he could depend on, it was money. Coming from a wealthy family, Mike had money for whatever he wanted. When he was ready for university, he did not have to apply for student loans. Others might have to scrimp and save and fill out forms, but not Mike. He walked around that university as if he owned the campus.

In a few weeks he discovered there were secret ways to buy grades so he wouldn't have to study. He had registered as an engineering student, and most of those courses looked so hard that Mike decided to use his money to make it easier to get his degree. The underground system of selling answer sheets and tests was expensive; Mike learned he could get a C grade with no problem at all, but an A would cost a lot.

"I've got the bucks, so why not go for the best?" he asked himself one evening in the dorm. Then he smirked. "This is going to be easy."

So for four years Mike paid those who were in the cheating business on campus. As he marched down the aisle to receive his diploma, he felt so smug and satisfied. "I haven't cracked a book in four years!" he said to himself.

It all seemed so slick, so easy, so smart to outwit the university and all his professors. Now he could apply for an engineering job and start making his own money.

With such high honors, Mike landed a position with an engineering firm right away. The people who hired him felt that such a brilliant student could be trusted to carry on responsible work. In a short time Mike was assigned to build a bridge. The responsibility of such a project was far beyond him. For the first time, Mike realized that he had made some bad choices and was in deep trouble. That was when he came to see my aunt, who was a counselor at the university. He sat in her office, wringing his hands over his plight.

"I don't know anything about building a bridge—or anything else, for that matter," he confessed. "What should I do now? I didn't learn a thing in four years; I fudged the whole time. Now I've got this fat starting salary, and I can't fudge anymore. I know nothing about engineering."

My aunt sat there looking sadly at him for a while and then spoke words that must have cut like a knife. "Either you start all over again as a freshman in this university and be honest this time, or make your confession to the firm that hired you. Maybe they'll have some janitorial job, and you can start sweeping the place at minimum wage."

What Mike realized at that moment was the curse of the schemer. The cheater always cheats himself.

Rebekah and her son, Jacob, learned that many centuries ago, when they schemed to cheat Esau out of the birthright by lying to Isaac, the blind old father. While Esau went deer hunting, Rebekah planned to cook goat's meat and season it so it might pass for venison. Jacob would go in before the aged patriarch and pretend he was his brother Esau and receive the coveted birthright.

Jacob was an adult and ought to have known better than to try playacting while his mother did the cooking. He felt a little uneasy about the whole scheme. Listen to their conversation as Jacob complains to Rebekah.

"My brother Esau is a hairy man, and I'm a man with smooth skin. What if my father touches me? I would appear to be tricking him and would bring down a curse on myself rather than a blessing."

"His mother said to him, 'My son, let the curse fall on me. Just do what I say' " (Genesis 27:11-13, NIV).

That curse was real. Rebekah paid the penalty that all must suffer who try to build on a lie. Sin is never so terrible as when it seems to succeed. She and her son pulled off the little trick with the blind old father, but in so doing she lost much more than she gained. She lost her beloved Jacob when he went into exile. She also lost the respect of her husband. And she lost Esau, who could never trust his mother again. She lost her peace of mind, and guilt tortured her until she finally came to the Lord with repentance.

But the darkest curse of all was that she sent her favorite son into the world with the twisted belief that sin could be made to pay. Ignoring the law of sowing and reaping, she sent Jacob away believing that he could somehow be clever enough to reverse that law, that he could harvest grapes from thorns and figs from thistles. Living with that misconception, Jacob had to learn the hard way. He, too, was cheated. In the end it was only by turning with all his heart in deep repentance that he was assured that God accepted him. The story of Jacob ends on a bright note, not because of his mother's influence, but in spite of it.

Willie and the Bag of Money

Several years ago I read in a West Coast newspaper of a

strange accident that occurred during the morning rush hour. I saved the newspaper clipping because it reminds me that in the midst of the dishonesty, lying, cheating, and stealing in this world there are still some people who are true-hearted and believe in the golden rule.

Willie Greenwood was driving his car to work that Wednesday morning when suddenly the rear door of an armored truck somehow came unlatched. Out tumbled bags and bags of money. Coins and bills flew everywhere.

Willie reported the scene later. "It was crazy," he said. "All traffic stopped. People were coming from every direction. They were grabbing money and putting it in their pockets. Old people, young people, and guys in business suits."

The wild scramble brought out the very worst in people. Shoving and pushing and hitting each other, they lunged for the cash on the street as if it belonged to them.

"It went on for three or four minutes," said Willie. "I couldn't move my car because so many people were in the street."

Willie saw that the bags had the stamp of the bank on them. He stepped out of his car and grabbed a bag filled with coins to save it from being stolen. After the traffic started moving again, he delivered the bag to the bank. It was the best he could do. If he could have reached more, he would have done that too.

The bank gave him a thank-you letter and some flowers, but for Willie just the satisfaction of returning something that didn't belong to him and putting into practice the real meaning of being true was reward enough.

The Great Glider Flight

When I was a boy, I was most intrigued by the thought of flying. Watching the birds soar and swoop and dive, I just knew the freedom of being airborne would be the greatest fun. Since a small balcony extended beyond my bedroom, I decided to test the air from there. The descent was extremely rapid, and I landed with a thud.

"If I could use an umbrella as a parachute, I could go farther," I said to myself.

My mom's umbrella would not be a good one to use. It might turn wrong side out—and I would be in serious trouble. That was when I began scrounging around in the basement. To my joy, I discovered that some friends of ours had left their huge beach umbrella after a picnic and had not stopped by to pick it up.

"Just the thing!" I shouted aloud.

I popped open the big red-and-black-stripped umbrella and felt the thrill of soaring just thinking about it. The next thing was to get that colorful umbrella up to the balcony. I was afraid to take it through the house for fear Mom would ask questions. After all, how many people do you see taking a big beach umbrella to a balcony, anyway? So I stood outside and tried to shinny up the post and put it on the floor of the balcony. It wasn't easy, but at last I succeeded. I soon discovered that getting the umbrella to the balcony was a minor problem compared to opening it. The balcony was too small and the ceiling too low to get that huge thing spread out fully. I finally had to stand on the railing, point the umbrella out into space, and slowly open it by swinging it over the edge of the roof.

"I gotta keep it from hooking on the roof when I jump," I reminded myself.

My legs wobbled and my arms ached from holding the umbrella in such an awkward position, but I was determined to try the leap.

The wind caught the umbrella and sent me sideways. I landed right in Dad's corn patch, not on my feet but in a sitting position. I was scratched and bruised, but my imagination was fired.

"I'm gonna build myself a glider and soar all over the neighborhood!" I exclaimed as I hurried inside to the medicine cabinet to attend to my first-aid needs.

Mom heard me talking to myself about building a glider, so I told her all about the planned glider-building project.

"Well, don't get hurt," she warned.

Hurt? Me, hurt? I just knew I could defy the law of gravity with my skills. This was before aluminum hang gliders were invented, so I would have to use the lumber scraps down in the basement. The wood might be a little heavier than the umbrella, but I was sure I could build a glider that would send me soaring all over the neighborhood. I told my friend Lowell the next day at school about the whole idea.

"Ya really plannin' to fly?" he asked me.

"Yep! Gonna soar all over."

Lowell had recently moved to our town from the prairie country of South Dakota. He was a slow-talking farm boy, but he soon showed signs of real enthusiasm as he watched me saw and hammer.

"How ya fixin' to git the thing in the air?" he asked as he squinted at the construction.

I'll have to admit right then it looked more like the wooden framework of a box than a glider, but I didn't want to talk about that part.

"I'm gonna have a place in the middle for my body so I can run with the glider for the takeoff."

In the center was a hole big enough for me to squeeze

through. The handles for me to hold while I ran with the glider were to be attached on the sides below the wings. At first I planned on a fourteen-foot wingspan, but I could only find twelve-foot two-by-fours. It took me a long time to ripsaw the board. My arms ached so much from the sawing that I had to quit and rest a while. During those breaks I gave Lowell more detail about my plans.

"I'm takin' a rope along, and when I get up, I'll drop one end to you."

Lowell frowned. "What fer?"

"So ya can pull me down when I'm ready."

Lowell was wide-eyed with wonder. He was actually going to be a part of the great glider flight. It was more excitement than he had ever known.

Even after Lowell left that afternoon, I worked hard to get the glider ready for flight. I nailed black roofing paper to the wing and tail boards for a covering. That evening at supper I was so excited I could hardly talk about anything else. But no matter how hard I tried to convince them, both Mom and Dad talked against my even trying.

"I'll show you I can do the same as the Wright brothers."

"But the Wright brothers were a lot older," Dad countered.

"That makes no difference," I said. "Age has nothin' to do with it. If they could get in the air, so can I. Ya just wait. Tomorrow I'll be makin' headlines. Boy Sails in Homemade Glider—that's what it'll say."

Mom and Dad laughed so long and hard that I just had to leave the table and go to my room to be alone. I was determined to prove them wrong.

The next morning Lowell was right on time for the takeoff, but his enthusiasm had faded quite a bit.

"Does yer ma and pa know yer gonna fly today?"

"Sure they know. They don't think I can do it, but they know, all right."

"Waaall," Lowell drawled, "my ma and pa don't think it'll work either. They sorta think yer sorta silly fur tryin'."

I put my hands on my hips and faced him.

"If yer gonna talk like that, then I won't let you hold the

rope. No grown-up thinks a kid can do anything, but I'll show 'em. Now are ya with me?"

"I'm with ya."

"OK. Then let's go."

My plan was to get a running start across the vacant lot by our house and then leap off the edge of the embankment by the road. At the spot I had chosen it was six or seven feet high, and I figured that was enough to get airborne. I could then bank tight and miss the line of fir trees to gain enough altitude to circle and soar right over my house.

The sun that morning struck the roofing paper so that it actually shone. It made me feel proud of my construction. The glider might be a little awkward and heavy, but I was determined to fly. I thought the wind might buffet me some, so a little heavy-duty framework would help.

As I climbed into the cockpit and started walking with the glider, Lowell started laughing.

"Ya look like a walkin' airplane."

I didn't bother to answer him right then. I walked to the far end of the field and then started running as fast as I could while carrying the glider.

"Well, not for long!" I shouted as I passed Lowell.

By the time I reached the embankment, I was nearly out of breath, but with one mighty leap I left the solid ground above—only to hit the more solid road below. Actually I was airborne only a few feet; it was impossible to jump very far with so much weight. I lay in a crumpled heap on the road. Wrapped in roofing paper and rope, scratched by the boards that had splintered, bruised by the abrupt fall, I could only lie there and moan.

When I failed to get airborne, Lowell ran across the field to see whether I was hurt. I glanced up as he peered over the edge of the embankment.

"Ya OK?"

"Aw, I'm not hurt enough to matter too much," I groaned, "but it sure hurts to tell my folks it didn't work."

Obviously there was a great deal more I needed to learn about the laws of gravity, aerodynamics, and glider construc-

tion before I could soar like the birds. How important to learn
those laws!

Harold's Free Fall

All of God's universe is subject to law. Can you imagine
what a terrible turmoil would result if it weren't? You would
plant some watermelon seeds, hoping to eat something sweet
and juicy, and up would come spinach instead! "Yuck!" you
say. "That is *not* what I have in mind." Thankfully, the law of
the harvest says that you reap what you sow.

The sun appears every morning in the east. That is a physical law God has established for our solar system. Suppose He
had no fixed laws about this, and some morning it popped up
in the north. Surprise! Then supposing that, rather than setting in the west, it wheeled off in a big lazy eight and dropped
out of sight back where it came from, only suddenly to appear
again at midnight. People would go crazy or get so scared
their knees would knock together. We simply don't like to
think of living on a planet running haywire.

If there were no fixed law of gravity on our world, you could
start to jump over a log and end up plowing the ground with
the nose like a mole. Or you'd start to leap a log and might
suddenly find yourself airborne over the trees.

Perhaps you have never thought of it before, but understanding the various laws God has provided and keeping the
Pathfinder law have similarities. Within the framework of all
law, life is enjoyable. When we break the law, all the fun
stops. The Pathfinder law is really an extension of God's pur-
pose for your life. Keeping it has great benefits—just as abid-
ing by the law of gravity, for instance.

A friend of mine overheard some sky divers talking about
all the fun they had in the free fall after they left the airplane.
Just listening to them talk about somersaulting, twisting,
turning, floating with arms and legs extended in the frog position, or diving in the delta position with arms tucked tightly
at the sides thrilled Harold through and through. The very
thought of sensing the freedom of space motivated him to sign
up for a course in sky diving.

"I've just got to try it at least once!" he exclaimed.

After he had learned to pack his own chute and had received all the ground instruction, the moment came for his instructor to go over final review.

"Now when you leave the plane," his instructor told him, "count to ten, and then pull the rip cord. You are not ready for any of that long free-fall stuff yet."

Harold nodded. "Count to ten and then pop my chute," he said to himself several times.

If the main canopy failed to open, he knew he had a reserved pack on his chest. It was smaller, but it would permit a safe landing in an emergency. As he climbed into the plane, he felt his heart pounding. It pounded even more when the pilot shouted that he was almost at the 12,000-foot level. Experienced sky divers can drop for 10,000 feet and then pop their chute at 2,000, but for Harold this sort of free fall was not on the agenda that day. He knew that in the first second he would be doing about 11 miles per hour, and within six seconds roaring at 133 miles per hour. As he looked out the open door, he felt a rush of fear, but he immediately braced himself. After all, he really did want to do this—at least once!

"Go!" the pilot shouted over his shoulder.

Harold leaped into space headfirst, and as he did, he rolled over on his back. From this position the sky looked so lovely with beautiful fleecy clouds and the deep blue beyond.

"Wonderful day out here in space," thought Harold.

All the time these relaxing thoughts floated easily through his mind, he was plummeting earthward. As far as he was concerned, there didn't seem to be any sense of motion. The sky looked all the same no matter how far he dropped. He felt so free and easy lying there gazing up at the sky. With his helmet snugly fitted against his ears, it all seemed so quiet, so peaceful, so relaxing—so much so he forgot to count!

Down on the ground his instructor watched in horror. Grabbing his big bullhorn, he lifted it toward the sky and shouted, "Open your chute!"

Right about then Harold turned over and glanced earthward. What he saw got his attention. His eyes opened wide. His mouth opened wide too. "Eeeeyooow!"

Reacting instantly, he yanked the rip cord, and out popped the colorful parachute—allowing a safe descent just in the nick of time. The fun of the free fall was never Harold's problem, just the sudden stop on the ground!

Harold may have innocently and sincerely felt that everything was just fine, but the law of gravity would not change to suit his feelings or sincerity.

When Harold told me about his experience, I couldn't help think of how important it is to obey the rules. Within the law we have all sorts of fun and freedom. Outside of it we have nothing but disaster.

The Principal's Pointed Question

When I was in the eighth grade, all the boys took a class in mechanical drawing. It was taught by the Broadview Grade School principal, Mr. Lowery. He was a good teacher, but that class came just before dismissal for the day, and late afternoon classes seemed to bring out the worst in me. I fidgeted and fussed unless I was forced to be really busy. My thoughts were mostly about getting home and getting on my grubby clothes, exploring the woods, and climbing tall trees around our house. The last thing on my mind was mechanical drawing, no matter how interesting Mr. Lowery tried to make it. His efforts were certainly commendable, but my thoughts were not about sitting on a high stool behind some sloping desk and making precise pictures of some assigned object. It was most difficult for me to concentrate.

One afternoon Mr. Lowery left the room temporarily on some urgent business. Apparently the janitor had run into some maintenance problem and needed the principal's advice. Whatever it was, Mr. Lowery was gone, and we boys were all by ourselves with no supervision.

Quickly I looked up from the paper in front of me, and my eyes darted around the room. Up on the front row was Jeff, intently trying to complete his drawing assignment. His head was a really tempting target. I looked down at my big art gum eraser and then slowly fingered it.

"Sure would be funny to watch this big eraser bounce off Jeff's head," I thought to myself.

The longer I thought about it, the funnier it seemed. Since Jeff was a somewhat serious boy, it might get him laughing. Maybe we all could laugh and break up the monotony. Maybe everybody would start throwing erasers. That really would be fun, fun, fun!

The temptation pressed so hard against my mind that I forgot all about drawing straight lines or anything else. Bouncing my eraser off Jeff's head seemed so much more fascinating.

Picking up the eraser and cocking my arm, I let it fly in his direction. It missed Jeff's head by a few inches. Close one! The eraser thudded against the blackboard, and I slid off my stool to go retrieve my bouncy ammunition. Just as I started forward I happened to glance out the window. To my utter shock, stories down, not far from the bike rack, stood Mr. Lowery with the janitor. The principal looked up at me at the precise moment as I was hurrying to the front of the room.

"Oops!" I muttered and quickly ducked.

In a half-crouched position I ran toward the front of the room to get my eraser. Somewhere en route I peeked outside and spotted Mr. Lowery again still staring intently in my direction. Rushing back to my seat as quickly as possible, I climbed on the stool and tried hard to busy myself with the mechanical drawing assignment.

In a few minutes Mr. Lowery returned to the classroom and stood in the doorway. To this day I can still hear his pointed question. "Doward, are you the kind of person who has to be watched?"

His question made me gulp. It did more. I began thinking seriously about how to answer to it. The longer I thought, the more I realized that I did not want to be the kind of person who had to be watched; I wanted to be trusted. Later I learned that God will have only people in the new earth who can be trusted. The redeemed will not have to be watched! Not ever! Not one in that vast throng of the saved within the Holy City will ever sneak around, trying to chip some pieces of pure gold off the bright streets or throw some of the fruit from the tree of life at some passing saint or angel. God simply will not recycle the whole disruptive, disturbing, self-centered sin problem.

The Pathfinder law is designed to protect you from being deceived into thinking that fun is outside God's way. By the grace of God you can keep the law and show not only people who know you here but also all heaven that you do not have to be watched.

Why Little Jimmy Stood So Tall

When I first saw little Jimmy, he was a freshman in academy. It seemed that most of the other boys towered over Jimmy, who looked frail and was small for his age. But before I left the academy after conducting a fall week of prayer, Jimmy stood taller than any of the others on campus as far as I was concerned.

It happened Saturday evening, the night before I was to leave for home. I was seated in the lobby of the boys' dorm talking with some of the fellows. Suddenly Greg, one of the seniors, came bounding down the stairs with some thrilling news to tell us.

"I wish you could've seen what happened just now up on the third floor!" he exclaimed breathlessly.

"Tell me about it." I smiled.

"Well, you don't know Sam Johnson. He registered as a senior this fall but was sent home for smoking. Anyway, he just came back for some reason and stopped off here in the dorm. Sam was swaggering around the halls and stopped off at little Jimmy's room. He started talking dirty and swearing—and then it happened. I mean it was classic. You should've been there." Greg paused and shook his head excitedly. "You wouldn't have believed it."

"Well, what happened?" I asked.

"Little Jimmy walked right up to Sam, looked up at him, and said, 'Now I've just had an experience with Jesus, and if you're going to talk like that, you'll have to leave my room!' Can you

beat that? Jimmy actually said that right to Sam's face."
"And?" I bent forward, eager to hear what happened next.
"And big Sam left! You should've seen the look on his face
too! It was somethin' else!"

Little Jimmy stood tall because he belonged to Jesus, the
Creator of the universe. He had learned one of the great
secrets of being a servant of God. He could afford to be brave.
He could stand up for principle and not be afraid of anybody,
any time, anywhere.

The Mystery "Angel"

The moment I walked into the assembly hall at one particular school, I was approached by a teacher. Since he was
smiling, I felt at ease. I had come for a week of prayer and
needed to get acquainted.

"We've got a little mystery going on campus," he said.

"A mystery?" I asked. "What do you mean 'mystery'?"

"Well, you know how kids get discouraged or down because
of grades or something happening between the students or a
disagreement with a teacher?"

"Yes, of course. You can't go through a school year without
somebody feeling low at times," I said.

"On this campus we've got a very upbeat thing going. The
discouraged and downhearted seem to find some gift-wrapped
fruit, a typed Bible promise signed 'Angel,' and a tiny feather
in their locker or just inside their notebook shortly after the
discouraging incident happens. Sometimes if a teacher gets a
bit out of sorts, the little encouragement parcel appears on his
or her desk."

"And you can't figure out who does this?"

"Not so far." He smiled broadly. "But the fruit, note, and
feather always show up at the right time. It's been a great encouragement to a lot of folk around here.

"Well, that's most interesting," I said.

I was even more interested when I actually saw one of the
little gifts firsthand. Since the message was typed, no telltale
handwriting could give away the secret. The little trademark
of a feather was amusing to me.

"It's a good mystery," I thought to myself.

For a few days I was too busy with speaking and counseling to discuss the mystery with anyone else. Then late one afternoon two girls showed up at the office assigned me. They introduced themselves as Carol and Michele. I motioned for them to come in to the office and have a seat, but they shook their heads.

"Could we meet you in the library right after everyone's gone home? They keep the library open until suppertime."

"Sure," I answered.

When I arrived, they were both seated at a table together waiting patiently for me. I started to sit down across from them, but they led the way to an adjoining room and carefully closed the door. I sat down and in a few minutes heard something of their backgrounds and their response to the week of prayer. Neither seemed to have any problem, but I guessed they were leading up to something they wanted to talk about privately. They seemed so cheerful that I hadn't a clue as to what was coming.

"Have you heard anything about the mystery of 'angel'?" Carol asked.

"Well, yes." I smiled. "It was one of the first things that was brought to my attention when I arrived on campus."

Then both of them began to laugh.

"What's so funny?" I asked.

"We're angel!" they chorused.

With the mystery finally revealed, we all laughed together. Of course I would keep their little secret because Carol and Michele were having so much fun. They told me how they listened carefully and watched for signs of discouragement from either students or faculty. Then they would search for a Bible promise that seemed to match the situation. They had saved for the fruit gifts and stored up enough feathers for a long time.

"The fun always begins when we have to sneak around and deliver the gift and promise without being seen." Michele grinned.

These two servants of God had made the delightful discovery that working for Jesus brings out the best in creativity and offers the fullness of joy.

The Miracle Man

The big steel door slammed shut behind me as I entered the state prison. Looking ahead, I saw steel bars and a heavy gate that led to a corridor lined with more steel doors and more bars. I was inside a cage. The guard behind the heavy window to my left nodded and then pressed a button that opened the heavy gate automatically. It clanked shut just after I walked through. I was now inside the prison itself, where the men who live there pay rent with pieces of their lives. Here people serve time—time that drags on and on and seems to crush those inmates who must live behind the bars and steel doors and heavy gates. I was now associating with murderers, rapists, thieves, and criminals of every description. As I walked down the corridor to the special room used for meetings, I clutched my Bible. I had come to help with some studies given to about thirty prisoners who came once a week to discuss what was written in God's Word.

That evening as I sat down, I whispered to the prisoner next to me, "It's nice to meet with fellow Christians."

He gave a snort and then chuckled. "Oh, we're not all Christians, mister."

"But I thought because you brought your Bibles and—"

"Naw," he cut me off. "Some of us just wanna get out of lockup, that's all."

I gulped and looked around the room. The inmates had indeed brought their Bibles, and they seemed interested. "Well, surely there must be a Christian here."

"Yeah, there's a Christian here. Ya see that black guy sittin' clear in the back of the room—the one with the deep scar down the middle of his skull?"

I looked across the big table and noticed a black man seated against the wall. He did have a marked scar on his skull.

I nodded. "I see him."

"Well, he's called 'The Miracle Man' around here, and he *is* a Christian!"

The inmate seated beside me told a story that left an indelible impression because it revealed the meaning of becoming a true servant of God.

This black inmate had accepted Jesus as his Saviour while inside the prison. He was baptized under armed guard right inside the prison. The prison officials did not feel it was safe in allowing him to be baptized in some church baptistry or river. His criminal record showed that he had been a very dangerous man, and they were not about to trust some inmate's word simply because he professed to be a Christian.

Prisoners on work crews are sometimes partially paid in cigarettes, and right after this man was baptized, he let it be known that he no longer needed or wanted cigarettes. Someone working in the kitchen thought that he should have those cigarettes. Unfortunately he misunderstood the situation and became angry at the new Christian. Grabbing a big paddle used for stirring soup in huge kettles, he waited for the Christian at the top of the stairs. Without warning, he struck the Christian with the sharp edge of the paddle and cracked his skull open as if it were a gourd. They rushed the injured man to the prison hospital, but it didn't look like he would survive.

"That's when they had a special prayer meetin' here," the prisoner seated next to me said. "We prayed the guy would survive."

I glanced toward the black man holding an open Bible at the other end of the room. "Obviously the Lord answered your prayers," I said. "Is that why you call him 'The Miracle Man'?"

"Not exactly. That was only miracle number one. When the black guy got out of the hospital, everybody expected him to go right back to the kitchen and get even with the guy who smashed his skull. But do you know what? He didn't get even at all. He just walked right up to the guy with the big paddle and told him, 'You expect me to fight you, don't you? Well, I'm not going to because I love Jesus, and that makes all the difference. I'm not mad at you; I'm praying for you.' And you know something, mister? Around here that's how they judge if you're really converted or not. If you don't pay back, then you must have something going for you. Jesus must be real!"

"The Miracle Man" not only had the evidence of God's miracle in healing him physically but also His miracle power in transforming a former criminal into a loving and lovable Christian. The first person to discover the second miracle was the angry inmate who stood at the top of the stairs with clenched fists the day when the black man was released from the hospital. He expected a fight but instead received words of love and a promise of prayer. That meant something inside the prison.

In the violent, revengeful world behind bars, the code is retaliation. Men sometimes make long knives called "shivs" in the machine shop and hide them in their trouser legs. When a guard isn't watching in the recreation yard, often called "the jungle," an inmate will stab someone and leave him in a pool of blood. Other inmates turn the other way. Nobody is willing to admit seeing anything. Sometimes, in the heat of revenge, an inmate will wait at the top of a stairs and trip a man, sending him to the hospital with a broken leg or worse. No witnesses testify in most cases, so they can call it an "accident." That is why "The Miracle Man" stood out in such sharp, loving contrast to the dark scenes within the prison. He truly represented love as a real servant of God!

Nora and the Rio Grande Express

Where Nora O'Neill lived there wasn't much level ground. The little weathered brown house she called home nestled against the hillside that reached upward toward the high mountains of Colorado. Below her house, the front yard sloped downward for about 500 feet to a broad ledge of solid rock. Right at the edge of this ledge was a railroad track, and just beyond the track, the ledge dropped steeply off into a canyon with a roaring mountain stream at the bottom.

During the summer months Nora enjoyed walking down the path to the railroad track and waiting for the Rio Grande Express, which came rumbling by shortly after supper. She would wash the dishes quickly so she could be down by the tracks in time to wave at the well-dressed passengers inside the cars. In those days when steam engines pulled the trains, it was always a thrill to hear the whistle blowing in the distance and then watch the great drive shafts churning as the trains approached. Watching the brightly lighted cars and the nice-looking people, Nora wondered where they came from and where they were going. She would wave and wave until all she could see was the black smoke belching out the smokestack in the distance.

One evening while Nora was helping her mother in the kitchen, she stopped and cocked her head. A rattling, rumbling sound came from the direction of the railroad track.

"What's that, Mother?"

"Oh, it's probably just the handcar with the work crew

heading back to town," her mother replied.

But Nora's hearing was a lot sharper than her mother's; it didn't sound the same as the handcar noise to her.

"It sounded more like a wagonload of coal being dumped to me. I've got a good notion to run down there and see what it was."

Mother sighed. "Oh, nonsense, Nora. You just want to get out of some work. Take a look at the clock. It's just about the time the work crew always goes back. They'll barely get to the station and lift the handcar off the tracks before the Rio Grande Express rolls by."

Nora didn't answer. She quickly finished her work, dried her hands, and opened the door to listen. Way off in the distance she heard the faint, mournful sound of the train whistle echoing across the valley. She knew the express would be making its swing around the great bend before it started the winding way to the ledge below her house. Without hesitation she ran through the twilight toward the spot where she usually waved at the train. Suddenly she paused. A dark shadow spread across the track. Running closer, she saw that a huge boulder, along with a lot of smaller rocks, had rolled right onto the rails. Most likely, vibrations from the handcar when it passed by had jarred the boulder loose, causing the sound she heard.

"What'll I do?" she asked aloud. "The express'll be coming in less than five minutes!"

She tried to push the big boulder, but she might as well have tried to push the whole mountain. Seconds counted now. Turning around, she sped back to the house.

"Quick, Mother! Quick!" she cried. "The oil can! The oil can! I must have some kerosene!"

She had already picked up a dry stick of pine along the path. Without waiting for her mother to help, she grabbed the can of kerosene and dashed oil all over the end of the stick. She had seen her father do this once when he needed a quick torch.

Her mother stood there shaking her head. "Are you crazy, child?"

Nora didn't bother to explain. Opening the firebox of the kitchen stove, she jammed the end of the stick inside. Immediately she had a flaming torch. Holding this high over her head, she rushed from the house and ran back to the track.

Already the express train could be heard pounding down the track toward her. Nora didn't reach the track any too soon. The bright light of the big engine was coming at her fast.

The engineer leaned out of the cab in disbelief and peered into the dusk. Right in front of him stood a girl waving a blazing torch. He yanked the cord to blow the whistle, but still she stood right on the tracks. He had no idea what danger was beyond the girl, but he couldn't run over her. He threw on the brakes, sending friction sparks flying from the wheels. At the very last moment, Nora leaped aside as the engine rolled around the curve. It kept on rolling until the cowcatcher nudged the big boulder and stopped.

The engineer leaped from the cab and took in the situation in a glance. Passengers poured out of the cars and gathered around.

"What's the matter?" they asked.

"Well, take a look at that boulder and where the cowcatcher is, and you'll know what's the matter," the engineer said as he pointed toward the front of the engine. "If this girl hadn't signaled me in time, the train would have plunged into the canyon, and we'd all have been killed!"

Now everyone crowded around Nora. She received a lot of hugs and kisses as the passengers kept thanking her again and again. In a short time the passengers took up a collection and handed Nora more money than she had ever seen before.

"But—but—I didn't do it for money!" Nora pleaded. "And, besides, it wasn't anything to do at all. It's not worth this much money."

The conductor patted Nora's shoulder. "You've saved a lot of lives this evening. None of us will ever be able to repay you enough."

After the work crew removed the boulder and the train carrying all of the grateful passengers moved on, Nora lay awake thinking about all the excitement and what had happened.

She hadn't signaled the train for money or for glory; she did it because she cared about people.

Seventy Miles for an Enemy

Being a friend to man—caring about people—does not mean being nice only to your friends. Over two hundred years ago something happened during the Revolutionary War that can help us understand a little better what Jesus meant by His words, "Love your enemies, bless them that curse you, do good to them that hate you, and pray for them which despitefully use you, and persecute you; that ye may be the children of your Father which is in heaven" (Matthew 5:44, 45).

In those days Baptists were often persecuted and despised. A Baptist preacher named Peter Miller living in Ephrata, Pennsylvania, found life very hard, mainly because of one individual in town. Michael Whittman was an evil-minded man who did everything possible to oppose Peter Miller. He hated the preacher and talked against him as often as he could, trying his best to turn people against this minister of the gospel.

Then one day Peter Miller heard the startling news that Michael had been arrested and tried for treason. Because he had secretly joined the British side, Michael was sentenced to death. Peter didn't rejoice when he heard the news. Instead, he put on his coat and began walking the seventy long miles to Philadelphia to see his friend George Washington about the matter.

When he was finally ushered in to see General Washington, Peter Miller came right to the point. "I came to plead for the life of Michael Whittman."

George Washington shook his head sadly. "No, Peter, I can't grant you the life of your friend. He is a traitor to this country."

"My friend!" exclaimed Peter. "Michael Whittman is not my friend; he is my bitterest enemy!"

"What?" Washington exclaimed. "You've walked seventy miles to save the life of an enemy?"

"Yes."

"Well, that puts your request in a different light. I promise to grant Michael Whittman a pardon."

And George Washington, true to his word, pardoned and released Michael Whittman. Imagine the scene as the preacher led his hardhearted enemy back to his home in Ephrata. But something happened to Michael Whittman. When Peter Miller saved him from the gallows, his hard heart softened, and he became a real friend. The grace of God had already changed Peter's heart to look on his enemy as Jesus would and, in the process, transform Michael Whittman too.

Four Special Life Jackets

Of all the dangerous routes to get men and equipment into combat during World War II, none could quite compare with the great circle route in the North Atlantic. The heavily loaded troopships would head north out of the eastern seaports, pass by Newfoundland, and then swing toward England. The Nazi government was determined to stop as much shipping as possible. They sent out submarines called U-boats that operated in "wolf packs," hunting targets to sink with their deadly torpedoes. The Nazis were so successful in destroying ships and those on board that the route was nicknamed Torpedo Junction.

Late in January 1943, the S.S. *Dorchester* tugged at her moorings in New York harbor. The small ship was once a luxury coastal liner, but now all luxury was replaced by rows of bunks four high to now accommodate as many men as possible. The ship was old and tired; rust poked through the gray paint everywhere you looked. The men called the *Dorchester* a "rust bucket" and felt cheated they had to use it for transport to England. With the top speed of ten knots, it would be no match for the speedy Nazi U-boats lurking in the cold waters of the North Atlantic. When the *Dorchester* finally left the New York harbor and joined the other ships, it was seventh and last in the convoy, laboring every bit of the way to keep up.

Four of the 904 men aboard the ship were chaplains, two Protestants, one Roman Catholic, and one Jewish rabbi. These four had a meeting with destiny. They would show what being a friend to man was all about.

After leaving Newfoundland the convoy headed into the danger zone. The weather grew bitterly cold. Ice began forming on the ships, making progress even slower. It was unsafe to be above in the frigid arctic weather, and the men felt trapped in their bunks, knowing they could be sunk by some U-boat torpedo. The tension continued to mount as the *Dorchester* rose and fell in the high seas.

The four chaplains talked to the men, trying to bring them courage. These four, Fox, Goode, Poling, and Washington, had heard the men quietly sobbing to themselves at night. They had known that the men wrote letters home blurred by tears. They had watched as the men sat staring into the darkness, not daring to think of the dangers. It was their job to bring hope and courage to the men, and the chaplains did their best on those cold days and nights as the *Dorchester* slowly wallowed ahead in the Atlantic.

The three coast guard cutters escorting the convoy were little protection from the submarine danger lurking below. The captain of the *Dorchester* already had received a message from the coast guard that the ship was being followed by a submarine, but there was nothing else to do but keep going toward their destination.

About 1:00 a.m. Wednesday, February 3, a German U-boat caught the *Dorchester* in just the right position and sent a deadly torpedo speeding toward its mark. The explosion not only opened a gaping hole in the side of the ship but also broke steam lines. Within thirty seconds at least a hundred men were dead, scalded, mutilated, or drowned. The survivors rushed up the slanting stairs to the deck. Confusion and raw panic seized nearly everyone. Some men cried, some cursed, some prayed; but all knew they must get away from the *Dorchester* as fast as possible or they could be sucked down into the vortex when the ship went under.

Amidst all the confusion the four chaplains moved with deliberate calmness, doing their best to bring courage and strength. They helped men get to the lifeboats and then opened the storage locker for the extra life jackets for those who had lost theirs. Suddenly there were no more. Of the nearly 300 survivors, none can remember who was the first chaplain to give away his own life jacket. It doesn't matter. With the sloping deck awash—the four chaplains—without life jackets—moved closer together and locked arms as each prayed in his own way. Somewhere out there in the cold Atlantic, four men wore precious gifts that could keep them afloat long enough to be rescued. While the chaplains prayed, the *Dorchester*'s stern rose high in the air and then made its fatal plunge to the bottom of the sea.

It has been many years since that awful night, yet the story of those four chaplains who showed the world the ultimate meaning of being a friend to man still glows with the brightness of the stars. Their unselfish deed of giving away their own life jackets gave a special touch to Jesus' words, "The greatest love a person can have for his friends is to give his life for them" (John 15:13, TEV).

Putting Dynamite in the Right Spot

If there was one teacher in the Broadview Grade School who said what she meant and meant what she said, it was Miss Barkley. As the eighth-grade homeroom teacher, she was fair but firm. One class in particular taught me a sound lesson in being prepared.

"One of the greatest speeches of all time was given by Abraham Lincoln," she told us one day. "It is known as the Gettysburg Address. It contains just 267 words in ten sentences."

Then Miss Barkley went on to explain how Edward Everett —the main speaker that long-ago day at Gettysburg—spoke for two hours. The President of the United States stood up after he finished and delivered his stunning speech in such a short time that few caught the full significance of what had been said.

"You'll find the brief history and background of that wonderful speech in your textbook. You will also notice a copy of that famous speech at the end of the chapter," she said in her own crisp way.

I sat there relaxed. It would be no problem to read the textbook. No problem at all.

"After reading the background material, the next part of your assignment is to memorize the Gettysburg Address."

Now there was a problem. Memorizing was fine—up to a point—but in Miss Barkley's class that meant you had better be prepared when your turn came. She would allow you plenty of time to memorize something, but there simply was no second chance after your name was called.

Looking down at the Gettysburg Address, I felt I could get the speech down pat in a short time. The problem was that I had other things I wanted to do after school. As the days slipped by, that famous speech got less and less of my attention. In fact, I forgot all about the assignment. Homework came and went, but that speech was forgotten. But Miss Barkley didn't forget!

"We're all going down to the little assembly room in the cafeteria today," she announced one morning.

Obviously something special was coming up.

"Anything to get out of the classroom," I whispered to the person in front of me.

Why we all had to march downstairs to this room seemed a mystery, but when we were seated, the mystery was solved. Miss Barkley, with her class record book in hand, was prepared to listen to the Gettysburg Address! She had even invited the principal down there to listen too!

"Ooops!" I gulped. "I forgot all about that thing!"

Now my memory was most active. I remembered putting off the assignment again and again until finally it had faded from my mind. I slumped low in my seat, hoping Miss Barkley wouldn't notice me.

"If I can get through this period without being called, I'll memorize the Gettysburg Address tonight and have it ready tomorrow," I promised myself.

The first person called was a girl who poured forth that address so fluently that it made me squirm. The next person was another girl, and she, too, recited the speech without a flaw. Maybe Miss Barkley was just calling on girls today. That would be a relief!

Glancing back, I spotted Miss Barkley out of the corner of my eye standing straight and tall in the rear of the room. Right next to her was Mr. Lowery. Quickly I slumped even lower in my seat, hoping to blend into the roomful of classmates. I wished I could even blend into the woodwork!

"Jan Doward is next." Her voice burst like gunfire in my ear. What to do? If I didn't know the Gettysburg Address, maybe I should give a great performance as if I were Lincoln himself. I tried to act as casual as I possibly could. Very slowly I emerged from the slump, straightened myself, and walked with slow and deliberate strides to the front of the room. I turned around and grabbed my shirt as if it were the lapels of a coat. I had seen pictures of Lincoln standing this way and wanted to come as close to the pose as possible. Even though I desperately wanted to appear calm, my heart was beating so fast I was afraid everybody could hear it thumping. Very slowly, with a great deal of emphasis, and in the deepest voice I could manage I began.

"Fourscore and seven years ago our fathers brought forth on this continent a new nation, conceived in liberty, and dedicated to the proposition that I don't know the rest."

Then I did another fine thing. I sat down. Although the whole class roared with laughter, Miss Barkley wasn't laughing. Mr. Lowery didn't exactly seem amused either. Next came an awful silence that made even breathing hard. Finally Mr. Lowery spoke. "If you had finished the way you began, you would have been much better off."

Flunking that speech alerted me to the need of being prepared. Being prepared, not only for class, but for everything in life. Keeping the morning watch is one of those needed preparations.

Preparing for the Roaring Lion

Watching a lion while standing safely on the opposite side of a concrete moat or outside a steel cage is one thing. It is quite another to come face to face with one of these beasts without any protection. To look at those white teeth and listen to the deafening roar without a barrier between would certainly get your attention.

Lions don't patiently wait in the shade until some prey comes within reach. Not at all. Lions go on the prowl slyly stalking their prey. Now notice carefully what the following Bible verse has to say: "Be alert, be on watch! Your enemy, the Devil, roams around like a roaring lion, looking for someone to devour" (1 Peter 5:8, GNB).

Now the man who wrote those words knew firsthand about the devil as a roaring lion. Peter thought, at one time, that he was really ready to stand up for Jesus. He was so sure of himself that he promised Jesus he would even die for Him. Peter meant every word of it too! Although sincere, Peter was unprepared. Jesus even told him that, but Peter paid no attention.

Peter spoke up and said to Jesus, "I will never leave you, even though all the rest do!" Jesus said to Peter, "I tell you that before the rooster crows tonight, you will say three times that you do not know me."

Peter answered, "I will never say that, even if I have to die with you!" (Matthew 26:33-35, GNB).

Well, Peter did deny that he knew Jesus. The Bible record tells us that somewhere between 3:00 and 5:00 a.m. Friday morning, when Jesus was tried before the Sanhedrin, Peter buckled under questioning. He even cursed and swore that he didn't know Jesus. Before the rooster could crow twice, Peter denied Him three times!

What went wrong? First of all, Peter became too self-confident. The old devil hadn't roared; he just sneaked up on Peter, making him think that he was strong enough and smart enough to withstand temptation all alone. Second, Peter didn't follow Jesus' advice to watch and pray in the Garden of Gethsemane. He slept right through the preparation time, and when the devil roared with his temptation, Peter fell prey.

Many years ago God gave Ellen White some important inside information on Satan's secret plan for the youth. Take a good look at what she revealed for the young people.

The Lord marks out a way in which he would have them walk. He has lent them talents to be used for his glory, to do a certain work for the Master; but Satan says,

1. I will *countermand* the order of Christ.
2. I will *find* another line of work for active brains

and busy hands, whereby they shall serve me.

3. I will *eclipse* eternal interests before this youth, and

4. [I will] *attract* his mind by worldly interests, and when he is disappointed in one,

5. I will *thrust* before him other attractions.

6. I will *blind* his power to discern, that he may work against the advancement of truth.

7. I will *bind* him about with worldly allurements like the finest threads, whose power to bind will become at last like ropes of steel, and he shall be bound in my service. I can lead him where I choose, and he will not discern that he is in hostility to Jesus Christ, my rival, and disloyal to God ("Words to the Youth," *The Youth's Instructor*, March 23, 1893, emphasis supplied).

So there you have it. Satan has it all mapped out to countermand (or give an opposite order of Jesus), find, eclipse, attract, thrust, blind, and bind. He uses whatever is most attractive to young people. It may be rock music, TV, drugs, alcohol, or whatever else is at his command to turn the mind away from Jesus and His power. Satan knows that he must get your attention away from Jesus, or he can't sneak up on you. It may seem impossible to withstand the devil, and yet God's Word shows us plainly how it can be done. "Submit yourselves therefore to God. Resist the devil, and he will flee from you" (James 4:7).

That first part, "submit yourselves," is what the morning watch is all about. It means starting the day with God. By taking time to pray and to study the Bible to learn more about Him, you allow God's Holy Spirit the opportunity to protect you from the roaring lion. Satan knows full well that when Jesus died on the cross, Satan was defeated. He keeps roaring because he wants people to think he is in command, but God has said that Satan eventually will be wiped out. In the meantime, the devil tries to get as many others as possible to be lost with him. He hates the morning-watch plan. He knows that if any young person will take time for prayer and Bible study and discovering God's wonderful lessons in nature, God will give the strength to resist Satan. The weakest person willing to follow God's way is more than a match for the devil. That roaring lion will turn tail and run when you resist him, because the good angels will be sent all the way from heaven to protect you from his temptations.

Dynamite in the Right Spot

When I first saw the piece of property, I was determined to buy it if I could. High on a hill overlooking the Black River Valley in western Washington, the property offered a view of the Cascade Mountains to the east and the Willapa Hills to the west. We could see the snowcapped peaks of Mount Rainier, Mount Adams, and Mount Saint Helens towering high above the other mountains of the Cascade Range. The spot was so beautiful that my wife and I decided to build a Swiss chalet with a big picture window facing south to capture the sweeping view.

The only thing wrong with that property was that it was dotted with ugly, head-high, burned-over fir stumps. These were not just ordinary stumps; these were huge ones eight to ten feet in diameter. In the days before chain saws, loggers cut the timber high off the ground. These big black stumps looked like some horrible black monsters protruding from the ground.

We did buy the property and planned to build, but first we had to do something about all those stumps.

"How do I get rid of them?" I asked my friend, Art, who had done land clearing.

"You've got to blast them out," he answered. "Get yourself some dynamite, and I'll show you how."

In those days it was easy to go to buy dynamite at a hardware store. I signed my name to the sheet at the store, stating that I was going to use the explosives for blowing up stumps, and bought a case of 100 sticks of dynamite, plus a coil of fuse and a box of blasting caps.

Art was a good teacher. "You have to be very careful with the blasting cap," he explained. "The tip contains cotton soaked in nitroglycerin, and it can go off easily. This is what sets off the whole charge."

After preparing the fuse and cap, Art then showed me how to attach it to the stick of dynamite. "This is the one that'll blow it all up." He smiled as he held it up for me to see.

Carefully placing this one stick, blasting cap, and fuse into a hole he had already dug under a stump, he packed in seven other sticks closely around the charge.

"Eight sticks ought to do it," he said as he straightened himself and looked around. "You must always have a good place to go for cover before lighting the fuse. How about that clump of stumps over there?"

I nodded. After seeing explosives go off many times while I was in the army, I knew I wanted to get far enough away before those eight sticks went off.

Art bent over and lighted the fuse. When he was sure it was burning well, he shouted loudly. "Fire in the hole! Fire in the hole! Fire in the hole!"

I was already backing away and ready to run, but Art didn't want me to run. Slowly counting to ten while he watched to make sure the fuse was still burning well, he and I walked to the safe place.

"Walk, don't run," he told me. "If you stumble and fall, you could get hurt when the charge goes off."

That first blast split the great stump into several parts and loosened everything so a bulldozer could easily move it away. Art stayed with me to set off another charge, and then he had to leave. I was now on my own in blasting stumps.

We were still blowing up stumps after the Swiss chalet was built. These were far enough away that the explosions would not damage the house. But one day my wife spoke up. "We have so many visitors with children. I just wish you'd get rid of the dynamite stored in the old barn. I'll plant ivy over the rest of the stumps. Now that it's getting toward summer and warm weather, I think it's just too dangerous to have around."

She was right. Warm weather does change dynamite. A sudden jar can set off an unexpected explosion.

"OK," I answered. "I'll get rid of the stuff. "You and the girls stay indoors, and I'll make one final blast."

For many months I had my eye on one huge stump by the driveway. Every time I passed it in my car, I would say, "Someday, baby, you're coming out of there!" I had singled out this stump because it was so big—almost twelve feet in diameter at the base and very close to the driveway.

I brought up the rest of the dynamite from the barn and began digging under the big stump. Once I had the hole dug, I fixed the first stick with the cap and fuse and then started packing the other sticks around it. I started counting as I packed them tightly around that first stick. "Eight, nine, ten . . . fifteen, twenty . . . forty . . . fifty!" I crammed in fifty sticks! There weren't any more sticks of dynamite in the case! Then I reeled off fifteen feet of fuse to allow plenty of time to get far away.

I lighted the fuse and shouted the usual, "Fire in the hole," three times. Only this time I added to myself, "And I *mean* there is a fire in the hole!"

I'll have to admit I walked a bit faster than usual this time. I wanted to reach the top of Coyote Ridge, where I could watch the fireworks. From up there I could easily see our little chalet on the knoll not more than a hundred feet from the stump. I trusted that my wife and two daughters would stay inside the house. Whiffs of telltale smoke emerged from the ground. As the fuse burned steadily toward the charge, I had a feeling that the whole hillside was going to blow shortly.

And just about then it happened! A terrific explosion rocked the ground as those fifty sticks of dynamite sent dirt and dust and debris flying in all directions. For a moment I couldn't even see my house. But I blinked in amazement at what I saw. The stump barely jiggled, then settled right back down where it had always been.

I hurried down the ridge to see what had happened, the smell of explosive still heavy in the air. To my astonishment, a huge cave had formed under the stump. The earth had been blasted away, leaving nothing but a hole so huge I could actually crawl under the stump. But the stump still stood! The only thing that had been removed was dirt. I had far more firepower than necessary. I could have blown up a bridge with that much dynamite. *But it wasn't placed in the right spot!* I should have placed it squarely under that huge old stump so the power of the explosion could have lifted it right out of the ground. Instead, I just blew sod!

It was after this experience that I began to understand what Jesus was talking about in Acts 1:8 when He spoke about dynamite. Listen: "You will receive *power* when the Holy Spirit comes on you; and you will be my witnesses in Jerusalem, and in all Judea and Samaria, and to the ends of the earth" (NIV, emphasis supplied). That word *power* in the original Greek language is *dunamis*. It is from this word that Alfred Nobel took the name for the powerful explosive he developed, which we call "dynamite." So Jesus was saying, "You will receive the dynamite when the Holy Spirit comes on you, and then you will be my witnesses." That dynamite has the blasting power to remove all the bad habits, all the meanness, all the ugly things from our lives. More than this, the dynamite of His Spirit not only changes us to become like Him, but gives us the ability to carry the message of His love everywhere! That's what happened at Pentecost when 3,000 were baptized after listening to Peter's sermon. The dynamite Jesus offers does wonders for witnessing.

So why then don't we see more of this power today? Remember the fifty sticks of dynamite? I had plenty of power available, but it could not do the work that needed to be done because it was wasted on the wrong location. Unless you are willing to allow the Holy Spirit to lead you in your life, the same thing will happen. You can go through the motions of reading the morning watch, memorizing Bible verses, saying prayers, and doing all sorts of religious activities; but unless the dynamite of God's Word is placed in the heart, you will just be blowing sod! No change will take place!

How Connie Conned the Counselors

The long line of girls from summer camp snaked back and forth along the high switchbacks of the mountain trail to Snow Lake. The giggling and laughter of those thirty-five girls making the climb had almost ceased by now. When the girls left the bus to conquer the Cascade Mountains, they were in high spirits; but now the steep pitch of the trail was beginning to wear them down.

Bill and I were the only two counselors along on the nine-mile hike. Since we had made the trip many times before, we felt fairly comfortable in taking so many along. Little did we know how quickly just one of those girls could occupy our attention!

Once we reached the lake, the girls were ready to rest. The scenery up there in the high Cascades is always delightful. The dark blue waters of Snow Lake reflect the jagged peaks and snow along the western side of the rocky shore. And beyond unfolds the whole sweep of more mountains and more timber. Everyone wanted to rest and relax a lot longer, but Bill and I knew that wasn't possible.

"You've just hiked four-and-a-half miles one way," I announced. "Remember, it's four-and-a-half miles back to the bus, so we'd better get back on the trail. We don't want to be late for supper back at camp."

The girls slowly got to their feet and headed up the steep trail out of the lake basin to the ridge overlooking the valley. We had chosen a couple of team leaders to guide back down

59

the trail while Bill and I brought up the rear to help any stragglers. Suddenly a cry of pain echoed off the mountain walls.

"Oh! Oh! Oh!" cried a blond-haired girl who had just fallen off the trail, "I've twisted my ankle!"

We rushed to her side and bent over to examine the right ankle she was holding. She winced in pain as she talked excitedly about how much it hurt.

"You're Connie Peterson, right?" asked Bill.

"Uh huh, I'm Connie," she answered as she wrinkled her forehead in pain. "I don't see how I can hike all the way back."

Connie got up and hobbled around, giving us a demonstration of how difficult it was for her to walk.

"Well," I said as I bent over, "we haven't much time, so climb on my back."

Along the smooth dirt trail on top of the ridge, her weight didn't seem much; but as I descended to the rough, rocky switchbacks, Connie seemed heavier and heavier. Bill spelled me off for a while, and we took turns carrying Connie until we reached the wider spot on the trail where it entered the woods. Here Bill and I made a seat by grabbing each other's wrists. Connie sat between us, hanging on to our necks as we struggled down the trail.

When we arrived at the bus, the other girls were already on board and sprawled all over the seats in exhaustion. We placed Connie in one of the front seats and headed back to camp as fast as we could.

"We'll be shaving it close for supper," I told Bill as he drove down the mountain pass.

Just as we came into camp, Connie suddenly became very alert. "Oh, there's my boyfriend, Jordan!" she squealed excitedly.

All eyes turned toward a boy walking across the yard by the administration building. Bill brought the bus to a stop and opened the doors. Immediately Connie leaped out of the bus and dashed toward Jordan. She didn't have a trace of a limp as she sprinted along. "Oh, Jordan!" she called sweetly as she ran.

Bill and I looked at each other in disbelief. "I think we've been had," said Bill as he shook his head.

"That sprained ankle somehow healed marvelously fast, didn't it?" I added.

Connie had obviously conned us. Perhaps she could recite with ease and feeling that part of the Pathfinder law that says, "I will do my honest part," but she would only have been mumbling words.

Chosen for Back-Country Adventure

On another hiking trip to Snow Lake a couple of other counselors and I took twenty-three boys for an overnight stay. Besides acting as guide, it was also my responsibility to take movies for the summer camp. In the back of my mind, though, I had something else I wanted to do. Secretly I wanted to watch the boys on this backpacking trip to select the very best to accompany me on a week-long photography trip deep into the heart of Olympic National Park. This little hike to Snow Lake would reveal a lot about which boys would be reliable. I needed to find boys who weren't complainers and grumblers, who could pitch in and help around camp without having to be told everything that needed to be done. I was really trying to select those who would do their honest part.

Because I was planning to hike far back into the high country, I knew ahead of time it would be a tremendous adventure. I was also looking for boys who didn't have to be watched. The last people I wanted along on that backpacking trip were troublemakers who might start an avalanche or pretend they were mountain goats dancing along the edge of a cliff. I had a hunch that before nightfall I would have my team selected without any of the boys knowing it.

All afternoon the sun shone hot and sticky through a filmy haze. As the day wore on, clouds began to jam above the peaks, rolling into dark masses that told a storm was brewing. It was highly important to get everyone settled at the camp site by the lake before the wind and rain arrived.

From the ridge above the lake, I watched as the last stragglers made their way to the old rundown ski cabin with the caved-in roof. I stayed behind to capture a few movie shots with the last of the sunlight before hurrying down to the lake.

Suddenly I stopped. My stomach did a flipflop, and I felt sick. "Oh, no," I groaned. Somehow I had developed such a feeling of nausea that it was all I could do to stagger into camp.

When I explained to the other counselor how I felt, he managed to smile weakly and pat me on the back. "We'll make out all right. First thing is to get a fire going."

While everyone scurried around gathering firewood, I quickly began giving orders about pothooks, number ten cans, water, and peeled potatoes—all the while trying hard to keep from getting sicker. After the stew was well under way, I excused myself to make my own shelter for the night.

As I lay in my sleeping bag, I watched the fellows. Amidst all the scurrying around and activity, three boys began to emerge as real leaders. As sick as I felt, I couldn't help but notice Rick, Gary, and Brian as they helped direct traffic in keeping the fire going and getting the stew fixed for all the hungry boys.

By now the heavy clouds had banked tightly into the lake area, warning everyone that rain was due shortly. I had dozed off for a little while and awakened to a brief shower. It was obvious that we were in for a real mountain storm. The Cascades can be very beautiful when the sun shines, but with the wind and rain, being in the mountains can be most miserable.

Most of the campers were seeking shelter. Rick had come over to check whether I needed any help. Because he, too, needed to get settled for the night, I hated to ask him for anything, but he was so willing. He finally brought me some broth from the stew and wisely left out some of the half-cooked vegetables. Rick smiled broadly as I gulped down the last drop from his cup.

"More?" he asked.

"About half," I said weakly. "I sure appreciate all your help."

Rick didn't leave until I told him that he simply had to make his own shelter for the night. Gary and Brian were guiding others at the same time that I talked with Rick. Suddenly it occurred to me that these three were the same ones the camp director had selected as junior counselors for the next summer camp.

"And now I know why," I thought to myself as I snuggled down deeper into my sleeping bag. "I think I've got my team for next August's climb into the Olympics."

I noticed that I didn't feel as sick if I lay perfectly still. But about the time I made that discovery, a bass voice of thunder announced the arrival of the storm. Louder and louder grew the thunder until the ground seemed to rock. A blinding flash of lightning beside the old ski cabin revealed two boys in their underwear running for cover.

"Rick, Gary, and Brian wouldn't be doing that." I smiled. Not only would they have helped others, but they would have made sure their own shelter was ready too. From what I had observed I was sure of that.

Suddenly the storm really broke loose. I prayed for the protection of all the boys. Closer and closer the storm pressed upon us. Now the lightning didn't zigzag across the sky but ran along the snow-covered ground in an almost frightening display of power. My hair stood on end as the simultaneous lightning and thunder cracked about me in wild fury.

Although two other counselors were along, I was so glad for the three young leaders I had been secretly watching. Now I was anxious to feel better and to return to camp so I could tell Rick, Gary, and Brian of my exciting plans to have them join me a year later. The best people to take along anytime, anywhere are those who will do their honest part, sunshine or rain, storm or calm.

Pussy-Willow Nose

One bright day when I was five years old, I spied a big vase of pussy willows in the hallway. What an interesting display! Immediately I trotted over to touch one of the velvety catkins. Soon I was touching a lot of gray pussy willows. The longer my fingers stroked them, the more I wanted to pick one. Before I knew it, I had a pussy willow in my hand.

"That feels so good," I thought to myself.

Then another thought pushed into my mind. How would that nice soft pussy willow feel sliding right up my nose?

Without further planning I gave that pussy willow a little push up one nostril—sure enough it slid in place so easily. Another one might feel even better. My little fingers grabbed another pussy willow, and then I slid that one into place behind the first one. Now I had two pussy willows up my nostril. I picked a third and fourth, and before long I had one nostril plugged with those soft velvety pussy willows.

There was no sense in having one nostril get all the pussy willows, so I started picking more off the big bouquet and pushing them up my other nostril. My hands were going so fast, I hardly had time to think. It was so exciting!

Suddenly it occurred to me that I couldn't get any air. My mouth had popped open in all the excitement, but now I wanted to breathe through my nose. No luck. Quickly I turned around, leaving the beautiful display of pussy willows behind. Bounding down the stairs toward my mother, I screamed, "Mama! Mama! I can't breathe!"

My mother looked up my nostrils and discovered foreign objects that didn't originally come with her boy. She gave a pull, and one pussy willow came out. She pulled one out of the other nostril too.

"There, now, is that better?" she asked.

"I can't breathe!" I cried.

She leaned my head back and began pulling more pussy willows out. She soon discovered that they were stuck. In fact, it felt like those pussy willows were clear up by my eyeballs. Eventually she got all those pussy willows out. Fresh air at last.

"You silly, silly boy!" she scolded. "What ever possessed you to stick all those pussy willows up your nose?"

"I dunno," I sobbed.

"Well, I don't ever want you to do such a stupid stunt again. Do you hear?"

I heard all right. I also remembered with terror what it felt like to have all those pussy willows lodged firmly up my nostrils. The soft, smooth feeling simply wasn't worth not being able to breathe.

How often people think only about the temporary feeling they get from introducing some foreign matter in their bodies and forget the stupidity of what they are doing. When using alcohol and other drugs, far too many turn their attention only to how it feels and not to the consequences. We were given only one body, and it is our responsibility to take care of it. Nobody who ever bought a brand new car would think of pouring sand into the gas tank simply because it felt good filtering through the fingers and looked so neat going down the hole. Nobody who ever received a brand new bicycle would deliberately take a sledgehammer and pound on the spokes because it sounded something like music when they broke and the rim felt so great when it smashed. We wouldn't do that to any man-made gift, yet how many will take their wonderful God-given bodies and wreck them with tobacco or drugs—all because it feels good for a little while or because others they know were trying it too. How stupid can you get?

The marvelous body God has given as a gift cannot be replaced. How important, then, for all of us to care for our bodies! With proper care, our bodies were designed to last a long time! More than this, God has shown us that by following the laws of health, we are promised a quality of life all along the way!

The Bible asks a very serious question in 1 Corinthians 3:16. "Don't you know that you yourselves are God's temple and that God's Spirit lives in you?" (NIV). But what about those who persist in violating the laws of health? Can God protect them from suffering the consequences of their own wrongdoing? Notice the next verse. "If anyone destroys God's temple, God will destroy him; for God's temple is sacred, and you are that temple."

Trapped in the Wastepaper Basket

One spring morning when I was teaching school, I stepped into the seventh and eighth grade classroom and made a startling discovery. There sat Rosie, one of the seventh-grade girls, sitting firmly in the wastepaper basket.

"What on earth are you doing in the wastepaper basket?" I asked.

She grinned up at me. "I can't get out!"

"What do you mean 'you can't get out'? Class will start in a few minutes, and you'll have to get out. How can you study sitting there?"

"I can't budge!" answered Rosie.

"Well, stand up, and I'll see if I can't get the thing off," I said.

Rosie stood and, I must admit, she looked funny bent over with that wastepaper basket stuck to her. I gave a tug—but nothing happened.

"See," she said. "I'm stuck."

"I guess you really are," I said.

Turning to some of the bigger boys in the crowd gathering around this unusual sight, I told them to make a pulling "chain." Each was to grab the waist of the boy in front of him, while the first one gripped the wastepaper basket. I took Rosie's hand to pull the opposite direction.

"Now let's all pull at the same time," I said as I strained to lean back.

The boys pulled and I tugged and then it happened—with a mighty pop Rosie was free! She stood up and smiled, her red hair bouncing as she shook her head back and forth in joyous relief.

"That feels better!" she exclaimed.

Everyone cheered and laughed, but I had a question. "Now, Rosie, tell me, just how did you ever get into the wastebasket in the first place?"

She smiled sweetly up at me. "Like this," she said—and promptly plopped right back down in the wastepaper basket again!

Every time I hear of people finally freeing themselves from some bad health habit, and then turning right around and dropping into the same old routine, I think of Rosie. How often we forget that, once free from those self-destroying habits, we should stay away from the source of trouble. Some things, like aluminum cans, ought to be recycled, but recycling bad habits is most unwise. In fact it is downright crazy!

The Week of Prayer and the Boy With Zits

It all began during a week of prayer when I chose to talk about how the ancient prophets showed us how to live in a modern world. By the end of the week, I was ready to talk about Daniel and his decision in the dining hall. Either this young Jewish captive and his companions would go along with the menu provided for all those in the Babylonian court, or they could stand firm for the principles of good health given by God Himself. Fortunately, they chose a vegetarian diet and stayed clear of the rich, alcohol-laced provisions from the king's table. The end result was a marked contrast between the Jewish captives and the others. In physical strength and mental vigor they had no rivals.

As I was speaking, I looked out over the faces of those young people and knew that they practiced wrong eating habits. Suddenly I said something that really got their attention.

"You tell me what kind of food you eat and when you eat it, and I'll tell you what kind of person you are!"

I had a hunch this would stir some minds. As the week had progressed, I had observed a number of students nibbling all day long. Their poor stomachs got absolutely no rest; that, of course, affects the way a person thinks. Not only that, the students were consuming a lot of junk food at school. I could only guess what they were eating outside of school.

A tall young man with lots of zits approached me right after the meeting.

"Aw, you can't do that!" he exclaimed.

"Do what?" I asked. My mind was obviously not quite in sync with his right at the moment.

"You can't tell me what kind of a person I am by knowing what I eat and when I eat it."

"Try me." I smiled at him. "Tell me what you had so far today."

He took a deep breath and looked up at the ceiling for a moment. "Well, I ate a sweet roll for breakfast and had half a glass of milk. Then on the way to school I got myself a cola."

"Anything else?"

"Yeah, between classes, I got a candy bar from my locker and ate a half a sweet roll I had stashed away yesterday."

"Go on."

"Then later on I sneaked another candy bar and another cola. Then I had a—"

"Stop," I said as I held up my hands. "You're the kind of person who blows hot and cold. Sometimes you feel religious and want to do the right thing, but when you're with the other kids going the wrong direction, you'll follow them. You have no firmness, no ability to stand up for any real convictions."

He scratched his head. "How'd you know?"

"You just got through telling me," I answered.

The poor young man had never figured out that what we put into our system and when we put it in does affect our attitudes, behavior, and thinking process. He was loaded with sugar and was picking up caffeine from the soft drinks as well.

Care of our bodies means more than just food and drink, though. It has to do with getting enough sleep, enough exercise, enough sunlight, fresh air, and pure water. It has to do with trusting God as our best Friend, as well. Since He made us, He knows every detail of our makeup. If we keep in touch with Him and follow His directions in learning about our minds and bodies, we will certainly know real happiness. Trusting Him means abstaining from those things that are harmful and realizing that God never takes anything away from us to hurt us, but only to help us. He wants the best for us. He wants us to be happy. Believing that, sets our minds in the right direction for excellent health.

The Great Garlic Stunt

One evening during supper Mom and Dad gave notice that they had jointly agreed on something to improve my health.

"We've scheduled a dental appointment for you." Mom smiled.

Even though I was busy eating, that announcement really got my attention.

"You mean I gotta go to the dentist?" I asked with my mouth full.

"That's right," said Dad, "and I'll drive you there myself." Then he grinned. "Just think. Your first trip to the dentist!"

Suddenly the food on my plate didn't taste all that great. Too many horror stories about dentists had floated my way. The frightful stories circulating around school about smoking drills and shrieking pain only confirmed that I wanted nothing to do with the dentist. The last thing I wanted was to skyrocket upward and take the plaster off the ceiling when the dentist struck a nerve, so I determined to try every excuse possible to get out of the appointment.

Nothing worked. As hard as I tried, both Mom and Dad were determined that I should keep that dental appointment. About half an hour before time to leave, I was desperate. Suddenly an idea struck me. "Garlic! I'll eat garlic!"

Running into the kitchen, I opened the cupboard and grabbed some cloves of garlic. I was glad Mom was not in sight; she would have stopped me. Now munching on raw garlic is not my idea of pleasure. It burned in my mouth. It was hot. It was awful.

"But it'll be worth it!" I told myself.

Dad was totally unaware of what I had done and so was the woman who clipped the little bib under my chin when I sat in the dentist's chair. I was careful to breathe through my nose. When the dentist leaned over, I was all ready to give him a blast. "Open your mouth, please," he requested innocently.

I not only opened wide as I possibly could, but I exhaled as much air as my skinny body could muster. The shock sent the poor dentist reeling back as if he had been shot. Wide-eyed, he turned to my father. "Bring him back later!" he gulped.

I leaped from the chair and galloped out to the car, with Dad not far behind. "That'll not happen again," he told me firmly.

I could tell by the look on Dad's face that he was unimpressed. Never again did I try the garlic stunt. All those sweets I had sneaked when I wasn't home paid off with decay holes in my teeth. Not only did I have to have them filled, but I was subjected to a regular checkup too.

None of us are very smart if we try to duck out of a medical or dental checkup. Finding the truth about your health is caring for the body too!

Going Where You're Looking

Several years ago in a large midwestern hospital, an orderly was hurrying down one of the long corridors carrying a tray loaded with medical supplies. Physically he was in fine shape, but he had an eye problem. He was neither nearsighted nor farsighted; he was walleyed. His eyes turned outward, showing a lot of white.

A doctor heading toward the orderly was also in a hurry. The distance between the two men closed rapidly, but the doctor stepped to his left just as the orderly stepped to his right. Quickly the doctor altered his course, but the orderly instantly shifted in the same direction. It was one of those times when two people dodge back and forth, trying not to hit each other—except in this case they both were coming very fast.

Suddenly they collided with a terrific force. The orderly's tray crashed to the floor, sending the medical supplies flying all over while the two men slammed into each other so hard they both sat down. As the orderly picked himself up, he was obviously angry.

"Well, why don't you look where you're going?" he asked crossly.

The doctor straightened his white coat and asked politely, "Well, why don't you go where you're looking?"

That is a wonderful question. Whenever people look one direction but go another, they invariably set themselves up for a collision of some sort.

If we say that we are Christians and are following Jesus,

then people should expect us to be headed for heaven. But if we are really headed toward the world, with all of its dirt and drugs and darkness, we will sooner or later crash right into the reality of truth. Abraham Lincoln said that "you can fool all the people some of the time, and some of the people all the time, but you cannot fool all the people all of the time." And, it might be added, you can't fool God any time!

"Looking where you're going" is another way of explaining the part of the Pathfinder law that says, "I will keep a level eye." You have nothing to hide; you are completely honest. You could allow your parents to come into your room any time and look through all your drawers because you know they would not find anything of a questionable character. You could allow the principal or teacher to look in your locker without the slightest worry that something bad would be found.

Many in our modern society think it is clever to be able to look a person in the eye and tell a lie. But that kind of "clever" is in reality very dumb. It began with Satan, the father of lies. Back when he was Lucifer, Satan started pretending to worship God. At the same time, however, he was doing everything he could to overthrow God's government. Lucifer made a devil out of himself. The first actor, he pretended to be something that he wasn't, and those who follow his ways will eventually find themselves, by their own choice, outside the Holy City. God is simply not going to recycle sin. All those found inside the Holy City will be people who keep a level eye! They will go where they are looking!

Twelve Fresh Tomatoes

Both of Seattle's public markets were fascinating places to visit when I was growing up. Today only one market is left, but the Pike Street Market still operates much the same way as when I was a boy. Merchants shout their wares and do their best to urge shoppers to stop and buy.

"Get your fresh oranges here!" a merchant will shout.

And you will never see oranges displayed more beautifully. Looking temptingly juicy and all lined up row upon row, they beckon customers.

"The best bunch of bananas in town!" another merchant will yell. To be sure, the bananas on display will look delicious. When I was a boy, huge stems of bananas were hung on hooks suspended from the ceiling. The merchants would take a little curved knife and cut off as many as you wanted.

Most of the fruit and vegetables are displayed on sloping tables that extend clear out to the sidewalk or the indoor walkway. On both sides of the aisle every kind of produce imaginable is on display. Usually fruit and vegetables are sprayed with water to make them glisten. Just walking through the market is an exciting education.

One afternoon, during my high-school days, I happened to be strolling through the market. I hadn't really intended to buy anything, but suddenly I paused. Right in front of me was one of the most tempting displays of bright red tomatoes I had ever seen. They looked so plump and delicious.

"Nice-a-fresha tomatoes!" the merchant shouted. "Nice-a-fresha tomatoes!"

"I'll take a dozen," I said.

Without a moment's hesitation the merchant popped opened a paper sack with a sound like a small firecracker going off. I always thought it was fascinating to watch the merchants pop the bags when people bought something. Now he had opened one for me and quickly filled it with tomatoes from behind the counter. He rolled up the sack and extended his hand for payment. I handed him some money, and he quickly made change and went right back to shouting.

"Nice-a-fresha tomatoes!"

I caught the bus home and kept thinking just how good those tomatoes would taste in sandwiches. When I arrived home, however, I opened the paper sack and was totally astonished. Some tomatoes were about the size of tennis balls, some like golf balls, and then a lot of little ones—with a few rotten ones—thrown in for good measure. I had been cheated! I lived too far away from the market to make it worth the time and effort to go back and confront that merchant who had not kept a level eye. Come to think of it, he didn't look me squarely in the eye the whole time!

People without a level eye will always hurt other people. Dishonesty is no joke; it is painful to get cheated. So when you say, "I will keep a level eye," you are actually making a promise to be honest and straightforward at all cost. No matter how many others around are lying and cheating and being dishonest, you can stand tall and say with assurance, "By the grace of God I will keep a level eye!"

Break and Run

The trouble all began one afternoon when I saw some boys in my neighborhood deliberately throwing rocks at the telephone insulators. Jay Swanson, a troublemaker from my school, was urging some of his friends to do as he did.

"We're tryin' to bust the tops off these poles," he said.

"What do you want to hit 'em for, anyway?" I asked.

"Make 'em break. It's fun to make 'em break, that's why."

"Well, my dad says it costs money to replace 'em. He told me never to throw rocks at those things."

Jay dropped the rock he held and put his hands on his hips. "Well, well, you're Daddy's little boy, aren't you?"

I could feel myself getting hot all over. Jay loved to get into fights, and I had no intention of fighting right then.

Jay paused and spat on the ground and then slowly wiped his mouth. "Sissy," he hissed. "If ya can't throw rocks at the glass, what can ya throw at anyway?"

I was thinking fast. Then I looked up at the wires. My dad had never mentioned those specifically. "Let's see if we can hit the wires. That'd be harder anyway." Just as I said it, though, the thought flashed into my mind that even this would be wrong. Dad had told me not to throw rocks at all because they might miss my intended target and hit someone. Throwing snowballs was one thing; throwing rocks was another.

All of the boys had accepted my idea and started throwing rocks at the shining wires.

"Just listen to 'em sing," shouted Jay as he hit one of the wires.

I didn't want to be teased, so I picked up a rock about the size of a golf ball and threw it as hard as I could. Somehow it slipped from my hand and shot at an angle right toward the Casper residence near the road. Before any of the other boys knew what happened, there was a tinkling of shattered glass as the big front window broke. Suddenly all of us froze.

"Who threw that one?" several asked.

I could feel the blood draining from my face. I knew who threw it. There may have been a lot of rocks flying, but I knew which one went through the Caspers' window. Suddenly a very angry Mrs. Casper appeared in the doorway. I took one look at her, and before anyone realized I was gone, I dashed across the road and into the woods as fast as I could go.

"Hey, it was Jan!" I heard Jay shout. "Let's go get him!"

Breathless and with pounding heart I ran like a deer for cover, ducked under some brush, curled into a tight ball, and hid as far back in the dense woods as I could. I was scared. Now I knew how hunted animals must feel. Suddenly I held my breath. I could hear Jay's tennis shoes padding rapidly along the trail toward the thicket; I could tell it was Jay just by the way he ran. Pinching my nose and exhaling slowly through my mouth, I lay very still.

"He must have gone the other way!" I heard Jay shout to his friends.

I could hear him running away to join them, wherever they were. Once he was gone, I hungrily gulped in air and straightened my legs. Now I just had to get home without anyone seeing me. Crawling out from under the thicket, I ran out of the woods and down 112th Street. Jay must have spotted me because, just as I turned into the alley toward my house, he jumped out and grabbed me.

"I got him, fellas! I got him!" he crowed loudly.

The other boys converged on the scene and began hooting and hollering at me like I was some sort of criminal. Pushing and shoving me along, they headed me toward Mrs. Casper's house. The neighborhood dogs began barking, and some smaller children joined in the commotion. I felt so cheap and foolish that I wished I could just crawl in a hole somewhere and die.

Suddenly everybody stopped. I looked up to see Mom coming to meet us—with a very upset look on her face. By the time she arrived, Jay had let go his grip on me.

"Jan threw a rock and broke Mrs. Casper's window," Jay boasted. "And we caught him too!"

"You boys go home now. All of you," she ordered.

I was glad for that. Then she told me to come along with her to our own home. Once we were in our yard, she made me look at her. "What on earth did you run away for? Your dad and I have looked all over the neighborhood for you."

I shuffled my feet and had a awfully hard time looking Mom in the eyes. I couldn't speak right then.

Mom put her hand on my shoulder, and I can still hear her say, "Son, never, never run away like that. If you've done something wrong, confess the wrong, and make it right fast. But don't run away."

I finally found my voice. "I know," I said slowly, "I know now."

It was the most important lesson I ever had in keeping a level eye! I've never forgotten it!

Jay's Courteous Mask

The curious thing about that troublemaker, Jay Swanson, was just how courteous he could act around the teachers at school. Whenever he saw the opportunity, he would switch on the charm.

"Oh, let me open the door for you, Miss Williams," he would say so politely. Then, with a rush, he would open the door and stand aside for the history teacher to enter.

"Well, thank you, Jay." Miss Williams would nod with smiling approval at Jay's courteous actions.

And Jay's ear-to-ear grin would make us all sick at our stomachs. Not that the rest of us didn't believe in courtesy, but we all knew how smart-aleck and foul-mouthed Jay was behind the teachers' backs.

Door-opening and book-carrying were Jay's specialties. He seemed to have a knack for being at the right place at the right time when it came to courtesy demonstrations for the teachers.

"Here, let me help carry that stack of papers for you, Miss Nelson," Jay would say and then bound down the hall to Miss Nelson's side.

"How nice of you!" Miss Nelson would smile pleasantly. "You're such a courteous boy, Jay!"

"Oh, I like to be helpful." Jay would grin with fake modesty.

It was so disgusting. The Jay who was so courteous to the teachers was not the same Jay we saw when adults were not around. He could push and shove and trip and start fights with ease. Wrecking someone's project was fun and games to him. He also was very gifted in filling his mouth with water and then squirting it out in a fine stream to give someone a surprise soaking. He even stole a student's diary and then read it aloud to everyone in the room when the teacher was out of the room. Teasing and tormenting seemed a part of his life. But he was always courteous to the teachers, trying to cover up his bad habits and disobedience.

Courtesy must come from the heart, or it becomes as phony as a three-dollar bill. Real courtesy does not pretend. It comes from a converted heart that, by God's grace, is living His law. That is why courtesy and obedience go hand in hand.

The Case of the Mysterious Stranger

A long time ago, Seventh-day Adventist ministers would hold evangelistic meetings in huge tents. They would pitch these tents in the various towns and cities and stay for weeks, preaching the Adventist message. Since there were no televisions or radios in those days, people often came to see the big charts and graphs showing such things as the great image of Daniel 2 or the 2300-day prophecy.

Besides the big tent and all the colorful things the ministers displayed in their meetings, they had another method for attracting a big crowd. The Adventist ministers used the popular method of debating. They would challenge preachers of other denominations to debate in public some of the controversial issues presented in the meetings. For instance, one of our ministers might run an ad in the local paper with this challenge: "$1000 Offered to Anyone Who Can Prove Sunday Is the Day of Rest!" Of course, there isn't any Bible text proving that Sunday is the day of rest, so the Adventist minister would feel comfortable in making that challenge. It seemed easy to win any argument with any minster not of the Adventist faith. When a debate drew a huge crowd, that pleased the Adventists a lot. Big crowds seemed to make them feel good; winning arguments in public made them feel even better.

But there was one problem. Debating over Bible issues could bring out the crowds, but it didn't do much else. Adventist ministers could win arguments, but they did not win people to Jesus. They could prove points, but that did not make the message a part of the heart. That was why Ellen White warned the

Adventist ministers not to debate. God had told her that, even though the method was popular, it was wrong.

Ellen White wrote to one minister about his continuing to argue. He had made such a habit of debate that if anyone asked him a simple question, he would launch right into an argument. This arguing minister and three others were holding tent meetings in Oskaloosa, Iowa. The main speaker, however, was Eugene William Farnsworth, whose father was one of the first Seventh-day Adventists.

One morning while Elder Farnsworth was seated at a table writing, a tall well-built stranger entered the big tent. Two of the younger ministers were chatting together at the time and noticed this dignified gentlemen. One of the young ministers was George Burt Starr, who watched with keen interest as this stranger entered. He had such a kindly expression on his face that George immediately felt a longing that the man might accept the Adventist message and bring a good influence to the people in Iowa.

Right then the arguing minister walked into the tent and approached the stranger. The stranger wanted to know what the big tent was for and what the various charts and graphs meant. "We are Seventh-day Adventists and are holding religious meetings," the arguing minister said. "We believe the Lord Jesus is coming soon, and we are working to prepare the people."

"I am interested in that," the stranger responded, "and would like to talk with you about it."

So the arguing minister invited the stranger to be seated while he pulled up a chair across from him. George Starr and the other young minister edged closer in order to hear the conversation.

At first the arguing minister spoke kindly as he explained about the return of Jesus and the resurrection, but when the stranger asked more questions, the minister shifted into his old arguing, debating manner. His attitude was so harsh that George Starr and the other young minister were afraid it would turn the stranger against the Adventists. Usually the stranger would reply, "Well, that is right. Now what about this?" That would make the arguing minister even more defensive, even though the stranger showed only a kind, mild spirit.

Finally, after about an hour of conversation—during which the Adventist minister acted less and less Christlike—the stranger arose with dignity and turned to the minister. "You are no minister of Jesus Christ. You are a controversialist, sir!"

He meant that the minister just wanted to start a controversy, an argument. You would think that the arguing minister would realize he had been rebuked, but he just chuckled and laughed, "Oh, you can't meet the argument!"

The stranger didn't reply to the comment. He had not come to argue, anyway. "You are no minister of Jesus Christ. You are a controversialist, sir!" he repeated. Then, pointing to Elder Farnsworth still writing at the far end of the tent, he said, "There is your minister."

When the arguing minister again just laughed, for the third time the stranger said, "Your are no minister of Jesus Christ. You are a controversialist, sir. I bid you good day."

And with that, he walked out of the tent. George Starr and the other young minister looked at each other in dismay. They both felt so bad seeing just how discourteous the arguing minister had been.

"He couldn't meet the arguments!" exclaimed the minister with his same cold attitude. Then he laughed again.

Later, George Starr told Ellen White the story and how sad it made him feel that such a wonderful opportunity had been lost because of a discourteous attitude. He feared that the stranger might be driven away from the truth.

"Why, Brother Star," Ellen White said, "that was an angel of God."

"Was it? How do you know?"

"How do I know? Why I gave that message to that minister at the Minneapolis Conference and told him that the Lord had sent an angel to rebuke him for his controversial manner of labor."

We may not see angels visibly, but they are around us daily. They want to take reports back to heaven for our courtesy and obedience.

"Stop Tok Long Here"

In New Guinea and the South Sea Islands the people speak a language called pidgin English. They have their own local dialects, but especially for communication with foreigners, they use this mixture of simple English and unique expressions. It takes a lot of words to say a few things.

For instance instead of saying "violin," they would say, "Scratch 'em in belly, out come squeak all same pussy cat." Instead of "piano," they would say, "Hit 'em in teeth, out come squeak all same pussy cat." When the sun sets on Friday evening, the Sabbath-keeping Adventists say, "Sun 'e go down, God's day 'e come up."

An American visitor to the region was walking along the village path toward the little thatched-roof church one Sabbath morning and noticed a simple sign stuck in the ground several yards from the church. It read "Stop Tok Long Here." In other words, from that point on, it was time to stop talking and be reverent in approaching God's sanctuary. The lips were to be sealed to all common talking because now it was time to worship the great God of heaven—"Him Big Fella topside."

It might not be a bad idea to have such a sign not far from our churches everywhere that reads, "Stop Tok Long Here." So often these days real reverence for God is lacking that a simple reminder of what it means to approach God's sanctuary would fit nicely into Heaven's plan.

How embarrassing to invite a non-Adventist friend to church and have that person turned off by noisy, irreverent young people! That happened in the balcony of a church I at-

81

tended once, and I have never forgotten it.

This older lady had just lost her husband and looked forward to fellowship with us that Sabbath. Although she had a Roman Catholic background, this widow seemed eager to learn and was not prejudiced. It was communion Sabbath, and of all Sabbaths, this should have been a special time for quiet reflection on the emblems of God's love.

All went well at first; then about a half dozen young people seated high on the last row of the balcony increased the volume of noise from whispering to giggling and laughter. They were even making fun of the Lord's Supper! Several times they were asked to stop, but soon they would be right back at their silly, irreverent behavior.

As we walked out of the church, the widow shook her head sadly. "That was awful behavior in God's house," she remarked. "How could they do such a thing?"

Accustomed to the Roman Catholic setting of quietness, she was shocked when thrust into an irreverent Seventh-day Adventist church service that did not speak well of the faith of the young people.

How could they do that? They could whisper and giggle and make fun of holy things because they did not know God nor love Him. They could do that because they had no idea of commitment to Jesus. They could do that because they were wrapped up in themselves and their own little world of sinful behavior. They could do that because they hadn't the foggiest notion of what real reverence was all about. Unfortunately, they wouldn't even know what a sign like "Stop Tok Long Here" meant because they were so out of touch with the reality of God's ways.

Those Cozy Couples in Church

Whenever the boyfriend-girlfriend arrangement intrudes into a church service, you can always count on irreverence. Boys and girls who think they are "in love" can get so enamored over each other that they forget that they are in church to worship God.

During an academy week of prayer, I watched two couples

bouncing along toward the front pew. Since I was seated on the platform, I could watch the whole performance easily. They obviously had figured that if they sat far enough toward the front, nobody would see their cozy actions. Most of the other students sat farther back, and the faculty sat in the very rear of the church. This little foursome had figured right. Nobody in the entire school would see them when they were on the front row. But they forgot about the speaker!

All during the song service they snuggled and whispered their sweet little nothings in each others' ears. Their hands were all over each other. By the time I got up to speak, they seemed unaware of their surroundings. I stood up, opened my Bible, and paused, thinking that surely they would stop their foolishness. But no, they were totally engrossed with each other.

"If the couples seated on the front row want to make out, I request they leave the church because I intend to preach from God's Word," I said.

That did it! Suddenly they gained self-control! Sitting bolt upright, they dropped their hands in their laps and stared intently at the speaker. Those behind them began craning their necks to see who I was talking about, and the faculty quickly came alive in the back of the chapel. Soon silence prevailed. The staff sat down, and everyone looked toward the speaker and listened carefully. I had their attention now and could proceed with the worship service.

Later, three of the young people on the front row apologized for their misbehavior in the house of God. The fourth refused to speak to me all week, but that was his problem, not mine— he knew he had behaved inappropriately. There will always be those who make getting mad at the preacher a substitute for repentance!

Showing Respect

Since the young people in the upper grades of the junior academy where I was principal had never been inside a big cathedral, I thought it would be a nice added feature on our field trip to Canada. As we stepped inside the massive church, all of the students were awestruck. With open mouths, they looked up at the enormously high ceiling and grand arches. None of them had ever imagined a sanctuary so huge before. Everything was perfectly still.

"It makes me want to be very quiet," whispered an eighth-grade boy.

I nodded in agreement as my own eyes swept through the beautiful interior.

Suddenly the cathedral guide stepped up and carefully removed the baseball cap from a eighth-grade boy's head and handed it to him. "Let's not wear that in here," he said quietly.

Busy looking around the interior of the cathedral, I had failed to notice the baseball cap. But the guide had a point. This was not a sports arena. Although not a Seventh-day Adventist sanctuary, it was a house of worship and must be shown proper respect.

Several years ago while visiting a Moslem mosque in Singapore, I was reminded of the same thing. A sign at the entrance informed all visitors just what was required. No common talking. Modest clothing—no tank tops or shorts were permitted. This was a Moslem holy place, and they strictly enforced their rules of conduct and dress within the precincts.

All of us could learn from those not of our faith who uphold a high standard of conduct and dress within dedicated places of worship. We need to understand more than we do that walking softly in the sanctuary means much more than being quiet. It also includes the clothes we wear, the words on our lips, the attitude we show, the thoughts in our hearts as we show respect to the King of the universe within His place of worship.

Who Is on the Lord's Side?

Aaron was the appointed leader during the time that Moses, his brother, was on Mount Sinai receiving the Ten Commandments written by God's own finger. It was Aaron's responsibility to keep the minds of the people focused on the true God. That shouldn't have been too hard. They could actually see the cloudy pillar by day and watch it turn into a pillar of fire by night. They could look up any time and watch the spectacular lightning amidst the dark cloud on the mountain. Every day they picked up the heavenly manna to eat and drank from the stream God miraculously provided. If all this wasn't enough, Aaron could have reminded them of God's marvelous deliverance in crossing the Red Sea. But Aaron wasn't up to it. Instead, he actually built the golden calf and led the people into idolatry.

"These are your gods, O Israel, who brought you up out of Egypt," the people proclaimed. And Aaron allowed this insult to the God of heaven. He did more.

When he saw how happy and satisfied this made them, he built an altar in front of his image and made a proclamation. "Tomorrow there will be a festival to the Lord!" (Exodus 32:4, 5, NIV).

That announcement was heralded by trumpeters all over the camp. By now the Israelites were so excited about having a god they could actually see and feel that they got up very early and began their "worship." This "feast to the Lord" turned out to be a wild party of sex, drinking, overeating, and music—the kind of stimulating music that jars the senses.

The devil hit a winner with this. Whenever he can get people to mix their selfish craving with religion, he always wins. He still is doing it today. Bring in rock music, add some religious words, and say it is all "to the Lord"—and it will satisfy many people. Satan's easiest device to turn people away from the truth about God is to mix worldliness with religion, the secular and the sacred, the profane and holy.

A strong leader was needed to stop the whole cheap affair. God interrupted His own instructions to tell Moses it was time for him to get back down to camp.

Passing through the crowds of dancing people, Moses seized the idol and threw it into the fire. Later, he ground the gold to powder and dumped it into the stream that descended from the mountain. Then he ordered the people to drink the water to show them how worthless was the golden god.

Next he called for Aaron. He wanted a full explanation of why this idolatry had been allowed. Aaron did what all weak men will do under pressure—he dodged the guilt by blaming someone else. Then, to top it all off, he wanted Moses to think there had been a miracle when he requested the jewelry from the people. "They gave me the gold, and I threw it into the fire, and out came this calf!" (Exodus 32:24, NIV).

How ridiculous! Moses was not fooled. If it hadn't been for the prayers of Moses and the sorrow of Aaron for the terrible thing he had done, God surely would have destroyed him.

The people thought Aaron was such a smooth and pleasant person because he never seemed to get upset and always did what they wanted. People are still that way. They like the flabby leaders who give them what they want rather than what they need. The people's sympathy was with Aaron rather than with their leader Moses. But not so with God, who looks on the heart. Of all the sins He will punish, none are worse in His sight than encouraging others to do evil. We have far too many popularity-seeking Aarons around and not enough people like Moses, who point to the right path toward God.

Moses stood in the gate of the camp and called to the people, "Everyone who is on the Lord's side come over here!" (Exodus 32:26, GNB).

Where would you have stood if you had been living back then? Irreverence is still very much with us today. And while we don't worship a golden calf, idolatry has never been more popular. Young people worship idols ranging from love of self to love of the opposite sex, to music and fashion, to drugs and alcohol and entertainment. Before you can safely say with assurance, "I will walk softly in the sanctuary," you must individually answer the question Moses asked so many centuries ago, "Who is on the Lord's side?"

The Singing Escapee

One of the most exciting experiences I ever wrote about was the story of Walter Loge, the German prisoner of war who escaped seven times from Soviet prison camps to make his way back to Berlin. The air distance from the farthest prison camp at Makeyevka to Berlin is 1,120 miles, so Walter walked a long, long way home. And all the time he moved ever westward in his seven escapes, he kept a song in his heart.

On May 1, 1945, though, that song nearly died out. He, along with other prisoners, was doing forced labor deep in the dreaded Krasnograd coal mine. He was getting so weary of the terrible, long hours and the awful conditions that it seemed impossible for him to sing again. Yet he did, and that song started, of all things, with stomach cramps and diarrhea!

The prison doctor handed him some pills and wrote out a pass to leave the mine and go back to the barracks and sleep off his sickness. But once Walter was handed that piece of paper, which opened the prison gate, he realized it was a ticket to his freedom. The Russian authorities never did find out what happened to him.

The Soviets celebrate May Day with big parades. When Walter saw a parade coming down the street toward him, he waited for the right moment and slipped into the line of marchers. His sickness was gone now. Swinging his arms, Walter kept in step with the music. He knew some of the national songs and sang as heartily as any of the Russians. Right then he was glad to be identified with them.

Gradually the procession began to disintegrate. One by one, the marchers waved goodbye as they left for further festivities in their homes. More and more marchers turned aside, rolling up banners and taking them away to be used another year. Still Walter walked on and on until only a few remained. Never looking to the right or left, he continued down the road until he marched alone. He did not look back until sure that he was far enough away. When he did stop, Krasnograd lay in the distance, shimmering in the early afternoon sun.

Suddenly Walter Loge felt like singing something else. It would be a long time before the evening prison count, and he wanted to rejoice. He threw his head back and shouted from a thankful heart, "The blessing of the Lord has opened the door!"

The horrors of Krasnograd lay behind, the fugitive had plenty of time, and before him stretched the open road for miles and miles. He hadn't felt so happy for a long time.

In the distance Walter heard a train whistle, and as its prolonged wail died, an idea came to him. Why not try riding the train? It would be a bold move, but no greater than the one he had just completed.

Just then he heard another sound. Voices—young voices singing. He listened carefully. It wasn't the singing that arrested his attention so much as the music. It was not a Russian national song, but something he himself had sung years ago in a young people's meeting in his church in Berlin.

"I know that song!" he exclaimed. "It's 'Always Cheerful'!"

It warmed his heart just to hear it again, and he quickened his pace. By the time he reached the intersection where one road led toward the train and the other headed out into the country, he met six brightly dressed teenage girls coming toward him. All were happily singing while one strummed a balalaika. Walter waved as they approached. Their colorful costumes, black braided hair with ribbons, and smiling faces presented a pleasant contrast to the drab gray scenes of the prison.

"Mind if I join you?" he called cheerfully.

The girls laughed. "Sure, sure, come with us!" one of them said.

He held out his hand to the girl with the balalaika. She understood and grinned as she handed it to him.

"I used to play one of these," he said. "Let's see if I can remember."

He put his fingers on the strings and started strumming with the other hand, changing keys several times before singing, "Always Cheerful." Their mouths dropped open in unbelief; then they laughingly joined him in singing.

> Always cheerful, always cheerful,
> Sunshine all around we see;
> Full of beauty is the path of duty,
> Cheerful we may always be.

Walter had to sprinkle the song with a little German, but the girls did not seem to notice.

When they stopped singing, one of the girls looked intently at Walter, her black eyes snapping with curiosity. "Are you a Baptist?"

Walter shook his head and smiled. He wanted to find out about the girls, but here they were beating him to the question.

"A Seventh-day Adventist?" the girl asked.

Walter nodded his head vigorously.

Two of the girls danced around the group, laughing and clapping their hands. Then they began laughing together, their young voices rippling in high glee.

Walter thought he knew even before asking the question, but he wanted to be sure. "Are you Adventists too?"

"Yes, yes!" they chorused.

Walter had stumbled onto fellow believers just after escaping from the worst prison camp he had ever seen. It was too good to be true, yet there they were, all six of them. Everything seemed to be going his way. It was enough to be able to slip away from Krasnograd, but finding these teenage fellow Christians was like a delicious dessert after a wonderful meal.

When the girls came to a fork in the road that led to their village, they stopped. "Come home with us," they begged.

It was a tremendous temptation. Walter would love to meet their families, to sing some more, to eat with them. But he shook his head. "It would not be safe either for you or for me. I've just escaped, and the authorities will be hunting for me very soon."

The girls looked sadly at each other, then at Walter. He explained to them about his flight out of their country. He tried to tell them how dangerous it would be to stay even one night in their village. They understood, but it was such a sudden end to a good time.

"You pray for me, won't you?"

The girls nodded.

"My home is in Berlin, and I have a long way to go." He smiled. "We'd better keep that our secret."

The girls nodded again.

"You can help me," he said as he glanced down the main road and then back at them. "How do I get to the nearest train station?"

The girls all began talking at once, but he put together their bits of information and hoped he had them straight. As he waved goodbye, he called back to them, "We have a secret, you know."

They waved for the last time, and as Walter turned and walked away, he prayed. "I want to meet them again, Lord, in that better land. Thank You for letting me have this contact with Christian young people just this once. I will pray for them, and they will pray for me. Now I know there are Christian believers in Russia. Thank You, Lord."

What a glad thought that when Jesus returns, Walter could once again resume singing with the girls he had met on that Russian road! Until that happy day, however, he was determined to keep a song in his heart!

Why Jesus Kept Singing

No child or youth ever faced more temptations and trials than Jesus did. The devil saw to that. He did his best to try to make trouble for Jesus while He was growing up. If Satan could lure Jesus into sinning, then He could never be our Saviour.

For starters, Jesus lived in a town that had an ugly reputation. Nazareth was noted for its evil. And if that wasn't enough, His friends tried to get Him to follow them into paths of evil. His own older brothers and sisters gave him a hard time too. They constantly threatened or tried to intimidate Him to do as they did. They even urged Mary to make Him follow what they thought were the correct rules and regulations of the religious leaders.

The temptation to be cross and irritable was ever before Jesus, yet He did not sin. How did He meet all the evil things the enemy tried? The amazing thing is Jesus never used power that we can't use in meeting temptation. He gave us an example of just how to face the enemy.

First of all, through prayer He connected Himself with the heavenly Father. Through the study of the Scriptures, He was guided from His youth into right paths. And through song He was uplifted above all the trials and troubles around Him so He could meet any temptation. Listen to these words: "With a song, Jesus in His earthly life met temptation. Often when sharp, stinging words were spoken, often when the atmosphere about Him was heavy with gloom, with dissatisfaction, distrust, or oppressive fear, was heard His song of faith and holy cheer" (Ellen G. White, *Education*, p. 166).

Now notice that Jesus did not chose some silly love song or some popular ditty with evil suggestions. Undoubtedly, Jesus discovered from His study that Satan was the former angelic choir leader and would naturally pervert music to serve his own ends. So early on Jesus was up to the devil's tricks. If music could be such a powerful tool in the hands of Satan to lure people away from God, then Jesus would chose the kind of music that would turn His mind and heart toward God. He sang songs "of faith and holy cheer."

Today we have a wide variety of good music to choose from in meeting every temptation. We need not be discouraged. By God's grace, with a song in our hearts, we can meet any temptation and trial—any time, anywhere!

Putting Pizazz Into Bible Class

It all happened during Bible class one day during the first year I taught school. Since it was a one-room school, all twenty students could listen in on the other classes. Although I was speaking directly to my five ninth graders, I could tell, out of the corner of my eye, that Larry, one of the eighth graders, was listening too.

"Now if you really want to add excitement when you're learning anything from God's Word, you should try holding a Bible study with someone who is not a member of the church," I said. "I guarantee that'll keep you on your toes for sure."

Tom raised his hand. "What do you mean, 'excitement'? How can the Bible ever be exciting?"

"The reason it is boring to many people is the simple fact they are not sharing. Even if someone is interested in discovering things in the Bible, it gets a lot better when it is put into practice and shared."

Tom smiled. "Well, I'm game."

Bruce half raised his hand. "Ya can count me in too."

Suddenly Larry spoke up, even though he was supposed to be working on another subject. "I'd like to get in on that sort of thing too."

"When do we start?" asked Tom.

"I'll get a projector and filmstrips from the church and begin training you this week if you're really interested," I said.

Tom glanced around at Bruce and Larry, then turned back toward me. "Yeah, we're interested all right."

Back in those days the church used a small projector with filmstrips, so the Bible studies were easy to give because the texts and pictures were projected on a screen. But I wanted to make doubly sure that Tom, Bruce, and Larry understood the subject matter first.

For a starter, I used the prophecy of Daniel 2 with its great metal image and the stone cut out without hands to depict the second coming of Christ. Not only would it help to establish the truth of God's Word, but it would also point them to the hope of the second coming. The boys quickly caught the subject matter for themselves and in a few days felt they were ready to go.

"OK, we've got it down pat. So what's next?" asked Tom.

"Yeah, who do we show this to?" added Bruce.

I smiled. "*You* are going to find them!"

"Us?" they chorused.

"That's right. If I went door to door, most people would not want a Bible study. But if you went, probably people would invite you in."

" 'Cause we're kids?" Tom asked.

"That's it!" I chuckled. "It is so unusual that people would more than likely be curious to find out what is going on. Now on your way home from school today, why not try a few houses right along Main Street just to see."

"Well, I'm not going to the door by myself," Tom said flatly.

"You do the talking, and I'll stand right beside you." Bruce grinned.

"And I'll be on the other side of you," laughed Larry.

So that is exactly how the boys did it. They returned the next day all excited about the fact that they had been invited into the very first apartment they stopped at.

"She wanted to know who we were and what school we attended and the whole works," said Tom. "I can't believe she really wanted Bible studies!"

"First one, right off the bat!" exclaimed Bruce.

"She wants us back at 7:30 Wednesday evening. I'm already getting a little nervous just thinking about it," said Tom.

"Well, I'll turn the knob on the filmstrip projector, and

you'll do all the talking, Tom," Bruce said emphatically. "You are the talker."

I patted Larry on the shoulder. "And Larry will be ready to add his comments at the right time."

It is too bad I didn't have my camera ready when the boys came to school Thursday morning. Such excitement, so much enthusiasm for Bible study.

They crowded around me, all trying to talk at once. Finally Tom kept waving his hands up and down.

"Let me tell him. This lady that let us in was the apartment house owner. Got it? The owner! And she invited—"

"All the others living in the apartments too!" Bruce cut in. "All of them. Can you imagine that?"

"Must of been about thirty-five adults," said Larry, wide-eyed with the wonder of it all.

"And they want us back!" exclaimed Tom. "We certainly do have to study now! Oh, wow!"

I sat down and smiled, soaking it all in. Suddenly the Bible class was not the same again. They shared with the others all the questions the adults asked, and their enthusiasm sparked greater discussion in class. For the first time in their lives, they understood a little of the meaning of "going on God's errands." And that was exciting!

Kathy Moves to Third Floor

In the boarding academy where I taught, it was customary for the senior girls to occupy the nice rooms on the first floor. The juniors got the second level, but the sophomores and freshmen girls were tucked way off on the top floor. Living on the main floor was considered a real status symbol at that school, and the rooms were especially coveted for their convenience and spaciousness.

During the last year I taught Bible at this academy, a freshman girl kept getting into more and more trouble. Vivian was a fiery redhead who could think of more pranks than most and could throw a temper tantrum in a hurry. Nobody wanted to be her roommate. Finally the dean of girls had reached her limit with Vivian. Either a more mature junior or senior girl could move in with Vivian and help her learn to adjust to dorm life, or Vivian would have to pack up and leave. It was that serious. But the problem was not one junior or senior girl would think of moving in with Vivian! Suddenly Vivian found herself very isolated—a situation that created even more tension.

It was at this point that Kathy came to see me in my office. She timed her visit so nobody would be around because what was on her mind was very important.

"I think I could help Vivian," she said slowly. "She seems to respond to me when I talk to her. But I—" and her voice trailed off.

"But what, Kathy?" I asked.

"But I don't want to give up my nice first-floor room! It's taken me four long years to get that room, and I would hate the thought of going back up to the third floor. There's no way Vivian can come downstairs, so it would be me who'd have to do the moving."

Kathy was such a fine Christian girl, and I knew what she was agonizing over. All real Christians have to do this at times. Self keeps crowding for attention, and yet, at the same time, the call to do as Jesus would do keeps sounding.

Finally Kathy folded her hands in her lap and sighed. "I've got to do it. I've got to help Vivian if I can."

Kathy left her choice first-floor room and moved in with Vivian, who was so startled that someone cared for her that she cried. Having Kathy as a roommate calmed Vivian down and helped her adjust nicely. She and Kathy became friends, and the entire school learned that going on God's errands does not just mean holding a Bible study or doing something up front like singing. It means putting self aside that others might find Jesus too!

Do Something for Someone Else

One Sabbath afternoon at that same academy, I happened to be walking down the main part of campus when a group of students gathered around me.

"Do you have any suggestions on what to do for the rest of the

Sabbath?" asked Tim. "We're all just a little bored, you know."

"I can see that in your faces." I smiled. "Obviously you've already taken the usual walk somewhere."

"Yep! We've seen the birds and butterflies and flowers," laughed Frank. "Now for something else."

"Did you ever think of doing something for someone else?" I asked.

"What do you mean?" several others asked simultaneously.

"I mean, right now, right at this very moment, there are students in the dorms who are sad or hurting. Maybe their parents are getting a divorce or they are lonely or are having a hard time with their studies. How about seeing if you can find them and make them happier?"

The students all looked at each other as if in shock. The thought had never occurred to them.

"No, I meant it. Right now somebody could use a kind word, a little prayer, a little sharing of some of God's promises." I sat down on a bench. "Tell you what. I'll wait right here, and you scatter into the dorms. Come back in fifteen or twenty minutes and tell me what you found."

I sat and waited while they hurried off to find someone they could help. The time slipped by all too rapidly, and suddenly they began coming back with all sorts of interesting stories to tell. Each had found someone to help. It opened up all sorts of interesting opportunities that went far beyond the Sabbath. It meant helping someone with homework or moving furniture or helping load someone's luggage for vacation, and—most important—a new way of thinking. I hoped that by God's grace they could continue on through life with that precious secret that few seem to find—that in putting self aside and going on God's errands you find real happiness. Like the old Indian proverb says, "Help someone across the river and, lo, you yourself have made it!"